GIOVANNI GENTILE

Giovanni Gentile

GIOVANNI GENTILE:
Philosopher of Fascism

A. JAMES GREGOR

TRANSACTION PUBLISHERS
NEW BRUNSWICK (U.S.A.) AND LONDON (U.K.)

Fourth paperback printing 2007
Copyright © 2001 by Transaction Publishers, New Brunswick, New Jersey.

Library of Congress Catalog Number: 2001027890
ISBN: 0-7658-0072-7 (cloth); 0-7658-0593-6
Printed in the United States of America

Library of Congress Cataloging-in-Publication Data

Gregor, A. James (Anthony James), 1929-
    Giovanni Gentile ; philosopher of facism / A. James Gregor.
        p. cm.
    Includes bibliographical references and index.
    ISBN 0-7658-0593-6 (alk. paper)
        1. Gentile, Giovanni, 1875-1944—Contributions in fascism.
        2. Gentile, Giovanni, 1875-1944—Contributions in political science.
        I. Title.

JC265. G42 G74 2001
335.6—dc21   2001027890

This work is dedicated to the memory of
Professor Paul Oskar Kristeller,
a truly good man

Contents

Acknowledgment

I am grateful to so many individuals and so many institutions that it would be difficult to catalog them all. Nonetheless, several have been so influential that some mention recommends itself.

The work of Renzo De Felice, Ludovico Incisa di Camerana, Zeev Sternhell, Stanley Payne, and Augusto Del Noce has been influential on the development of my interpretation of Fascism, generic fascism and the thought of Giovanni Gentile. Conversations with Giuseppe Prezzolini, years ago, convinced me that Gentile's thought was central to Fascism as a regime.

The Research Center of the Marine Corps University at Quantico provided the facilities and the opportunity to pursue my studies as Oppenheimer Professor during the year 1996–1997. The University of California, Berkeley provided the environment and the access to students that afforded me the occasion of sharpening my interpretation of the work of Giovanni Gentile.

I am grateful to my wife, Professor Maria Hsia Chang, for her patience and intelligent judgment concerning my work. To little Gabriel and Charles Elmo, I am grateful for their being there.

A. J. G.
Berkeley, 2000

Preface

Several considerations contributed to the decision to prepare this brief manuscript for publication. The first was the generous suggestion made by Professor Irving Louis Horowitz and Mary Curtis that such a project would be favorably considered by Transaction Publishers. The second was that the manuscript would discharge some small portion of the debt I owe to Professor Paul Oskar Kristeller. Professor Kristeller was a mentor to both Professor Horowitz and myself at Columbia University—at a time when Columbia was one of the premier universities of the world. The third consideration is peculiarly my own.

During my years at Columbia University, Professor Kristeller was uncommonly generous to me—a student from the most impoverished sections of Brooklyn, New York. It was during that time that he told me of Giovanni Gentile's intervention—at considerable personal risk—to protect him from both the anti-Semitic legislation of National Socialist Germany and that of Fascist Italy. When Professor Kristeller found that I was considering a study of the "Social and Political Philosophy of Giovanni Gentile," as a doctoral dissertation, he offered whatever help he could. He felt he owed something to Gentile. To this day, I remember Paul Oskar Kristeller—and the way he spoke of his debt to the humanity of Giovanni Gentile.

For the purposes of intelligent laymen, all that is of little consequence. More than any of that, a treatment of the thought of Gentile serves to redress any number of singular stupidities that have collected around the contemporary interpretation of Fascism. Since the collapse of Marxist-Leninist systems throughout the world, some Western academics have chosen to attempt to recreate a "threat of European fascism" that might, once again, reanimate a popular "anti-fascism" among Europeans and Americans—to provide a rearguard alternative for unregenerate leftists unprepared to accept the notion that Marxism has shown itself to be nonviable, empty of promise, and unconvincing as an alternative to "industrial capitalism."

For these nostalgics, Fascism, once again, is identified as "the product of late capitalism." They seek to resurrect an interpretation that has long since lost all credibility, and has passed, unlamented, into history. Most of the nations that hosted significant fascist movements were far from the products of "late industrial capitalism." The first Fascism, that of turn-of-the-century Italy, took root in an industrially retarded environment, in a nation newly reunited, possessed of a traditional agrarian economy, and essentially innocent of an urban proletariat.

A curious "consensus" has emerged among the disappointed neo-Marxists of the West. They have chosen to identify Fascism, and generic fascism, with any form of real or potential violence: thuggery at soccer matches, skinhead obscenities, immigrant bashing, vandalism in graveyards, anti-feminism, homophobia, and "hate speech."

"Fascism" is seen as embodied in fundamentalist Christian beliefs, in anti-communist sentiments, in tax protests, in libertarianism, in sexism, in "anti-environmentalism," in the indifference to the abuse of children and animals—in effect, in anything deplored by prevailing "political correctness." There are "neofascists," "cryptofascists," "parafascists," and "quasifascists" everywhere. "Fascism," we are told, is pandemic.

All of this is fundamentally empty of any cognitive significance. Italian Fascism (and generic fascism) was, and is, an antidemocratic reaction to what were seen to be the impostures of the advanced industrial democracies—more frequently than not, by less-developed and/or status-deprived communities languishing on the margins of the "Great Powers."

Should one choose to seek out today's fascism, one is counseled to look to the retrograde former Soviet Union, and the reformist People's Republic of China. They are the natural hosts of a "resurgence" of fascism. In the advanced industrial democracies, one finds very little that could credibly be identified as fascism. One finds marginal persons, who have learned what "fascism" is from late-night television—acting out their clinical and sub-clinical personality disorders. They are the "fascists" reported by the mainstream press and their academic spokesmen. There is very little "fascism" to be found in any of that.

Fascism, however construed, is more likely to be found in "communist" China, than in industrialized Europe or North America. Why that should be the case can only be appreciated after one comes to understand something about the advent of Italian Fascism in Europe. It was Mussolini's Fascism that gave form and character to revolution in the modern world. It is that fascism that still has ominous meaning for our time.

To really understand something about Italian Fascism in particular, and fascisms in general, is to understand something about Giovanni Gentile. He was a Fascist before there was Fascism—and he both infused it with his thought and served as its conscience.

It will be argued here that Gentile supplied Fascism its justificatory rationale: the totalitarianism that informed Fascism's antidemocratic convictions. It was he who defined the relationship between the individual, any association of individuals, and the political state. It was Gentile who made obedience, work, and sacrifice, the ethic of a national community in developmental rebellion against what he took to be the hegemonic impostures of imperialism.

As has been argued elsewhere, Fascism was the rationale for a developmental dictatorship. Many intellectual currents contributed to its articulation. Nationalism was one. Futurism was another. National Syndicalism yet another. Gentilean Actualism (as his philosophy was identified) was one as well. Fascism was all of these. It expressed the doctrine of a less-developed, status-deprived country's reaction against all the weight of the nineteenth and twentieth century. It was the paradigm of what we can expect in the twenty-first century's response, on the part of less-developed and status-deprived nations, to the hegemonic "globalization" of the industrialized democracies.

Gentile's Actualism was, in part, a reaction to his time and his circumstances. As such, he was a voice for turn of the twentieth-century Italy. In our own time he could only have been silent. The Italy of the twenty-first century is deaf to the idealism, the voluntarism, the dedication, and the sacrifice until death, that his Actualism sought to foster. The fact is that the entire Western world is indifferent to all of that. In the industrialized democracies, our time is a time of profligate abundance and exalted status. Few in the industrialized democracies understand the anguish of post–World War I Italy—or of post–Soviet Russia or post-Maoist China. We have little idea of what political sentiments move those in Eastern Europe, the Balkans, or in East or Southern Asia. We cannot understand why the sacrifice and the moral imperatives of Gentile might engage the sentiment of peoples—

in the marginal economies of the world—who have never read a word of his works.

The thought of Giovanni Gentile is no longer of any political consequence to most of the peoples of Europe. They have long since transcended the stage of development where commitment, dedication, sacrifice, frugality, obedience, and unremitting labor were functional necessities for the restoration of a broken "Fatherland." One will find remnants of such concerns in the talk of the politically active in the Balkans and in nationalist Russia. There is talk of these virtues in post-Maoist China. Perhaps there will be talk of such things in tomorrow's Africa. Whatever the case, the thought of Giovanni Gentile tells us a great deal concerning what we have learned about the talk of revolutionaries in the twentieth, and what we can expect to hear in their talk in the twenty-first. Whatever else it was, Gentile's Actualism was the philosophy of a community in a desperate search for its own renewal, identity, and place, in a world of dominant industrial powers.

Whether or not thinkers of less developed communities know anything of Gentile's Actualism, I am convinced that his emphasis on voluntarism, obedience, self-realization, the identification of the individual with the state, charismatic leadership and the role of elites in development, are all elements of the reactive nationalism of less-developed nations in their confrontation with those more developed.

At least for those reasons, the study of Gentile's Actualism is a matter of practical importance. Its analogue will be found in the thought of revolutionaries throughout the less-developed world. While Marxism-Leninism has passed, quietly, into history—fascism has emerged as something with which the advanced industrial democracies will have to contend—not in industrially developed environments, but in the less-developed periphery.

A. James Gregor
Berkeley, 2000

1

The Life of Giovanni Gentile

Giovanni Gentile was born in Castelvetrano, Sicily, of Giovanni and Theresa Curti on the 30th of May 1875 and completed his elementary schooling in his native township. In nearby Trapani, he attended the *ginnasio* and the *liceo* before being admitted to the Scuola normale superiore of Pisa, where he graduated with a degree in philosophy in 1897. His thesis involved treatment of the ideas of "Rosmini and Gioberti."[1] From Pisa, he undertook advanced studies at the University of Florence. From there, he commenced his teaching career in the lyceum at Campobasso and Naples (1898–1906).

From 1896 forward, Gentile developed an intellectual friendship with Benedetto Croce and in 1903 conducted a course of instruction at the University of Naples on the subject, "The Rebirth of Idealism"—thereby commencing a philosophical program that would occupy him for the remainder of his life. In 1906, Gentile was called to the University of Palermo to fill the chair in the history of philosophy—to. remain there until 1914, when he was invited to Pisa, there to take up the responsibilities of the chair of his former teacher Donato Jaja.

Jaja had been a student of the Italian neo-Hegelian idealist, Bertrando Spaventa (1817–1883). Through Jaja, Spaventa was to exercise significant influence on the thought of Gentile.[2]

In 1917, Gentile returned to the University of Rome and in 1925, founded there the School of Philosophy. In 1920, Gentile founded his own philosophical review, *Giornale critico della filosofia italiana*. He remained a professor of philosophy at the University of Rome until shortly before his death.

In October 1922, immediately after the Fascist March on Rome,

1

Gentile, a Nationalist and a Liberal, was invited by Benito Mussolini to serve in his first cabinet as Minister of Public Instruction—a position Gentile held until July of 1924. During this period, on the 31st of May 1923, Gentile formally applied for membership in the Partito nazionale fascista.[3] During his twenty months of service in the new administration as minister, Gentile initiated a reform in public instruction—the first organic reform of public education since the Casati law of 1859. On the 5th of November 1923, Gentile was appointed senator of the realm, a representative in the Upper House of the Italian Parliament. In that same year, he founded *L'Educazione politica*, which, in 1925, became the journal of the Istituto nazionale fascista di cultura. Between 1927 and 1933, the journal was entitled *Educazione fascista* and after 1933, *Civiltà fascista*. From 1929 through 1930, Gentile was director of *Bibliografia fascista*—a systematic bibliographical collection of literature devoted to Fascism.

Immediately upon his resignation from his ministerial post in 1924, Gentile served, at Mussolini's invitation, as president of the "Commission of Fifteen," and subsequently the "Commission of Eighteen," devoted to the constitutional reform that followed the accession of Fascism to power. The reform focused, basically, on the new role the prime minister, as head of state, would play in the new Fascist government, and the problem of how corporativist legislation could be accommodated by the Albertine Constitution—the constitutional instrument by which Italy had been governed since its unification.

From the very commencement of the Fascist regime,[4] Gentile's public service both expanded and became increasingly complex. He served as president of the Superior Council of Public Instruction in the years between 1926 and 1928. He was a member of the Grand Council of Fascism from 1923 to 1924, and from 1925 through 1929, first as minister of the cabinet, and then as president of the Istituto nazionale fascista di cultura, which he founded in 1925 and over which he presided until 1937.[5] He served as the president of the Italian Institute of Germanic Studies from 1934 and of the Institute for the Study of the Middle and Extreme Orient from 1933 until his death in 1944.

From 1925 until 1944, Gentile supervised the publication of the *Enciclopedia Italiana*, serving as its scientific director. It was during that period, and in that capacity, that Gentile was charged by Mussolini, over the objections of the Roman Catholic Church[6], to write the first part of the offical "*Dottrina del fascismo*," that appeared as an insert in volume XIV of the *Enciclopedia Italiana* in June 1932. The "Doctrine" was described as "the fundamental and synthetic foundation for any study, historic or theoretical, concerning the development, thought and practice of Fascism."[7]

The first part of the *Dottrina*, written by Gentile, was a summary statement of his Actualism, the neo-Hegelian philosophy he had formulated. Although almost entirely written by Gentile, the first part, the "Fundamental Ideas," appeared over the name of Mussolini—thereby endowing it with an official character.[8] The relationship of Gentile's philosophy and Fascism was thereby formally established. As a consequence, among the orthodox and until the end of the regime, Fascism was described, in its propaganda literature, as a "luminous historic example" of Gentilean Actualism.[9]

Throughout the history of Fascism, Gentile was among the most prominent of the Italian intellectuals who identified with Fascism, largely without qualification—until the affiliation with National Socialist Germany became intimate in the mid-thirties. At the end of the regime—when Fascism was confined to northern Italy—he was among the few intellectuals who committed themselves to its service. Gentile volunteered to serve Republican Fascism, the Fascism that survived Mussolini's dismissal by Vittorio Emanuele III, the king of Italy, on 23 July 1943.

After the dismissal of Mussolini on that date and the subsequent collapse of the Fascist regime, General Pietro Badoglio assumed responsibility for the nation—and proceeded to surrender to the Allied powers—to subsequently seek "cobelligerancy" status with them in the war against National Socialist Germany (and, by implication, with the Republican Fascist regime[10] that established itself in the German-occupied north of the Italian peninsula).

In the Repubblica di Salò—the Fascist republican government in northern Italy that prevailed between 1943 and the end of the Second World War in April-May 1945—Gentile served, until his death in April 1944, as president of the Accademia d'Italia, Italy's foremost intellectual institution. In effect, from 1922 until his death in 1944, Gentile served Fascism as one of its principal intellectual spokesmen—providing it not only vindication, but its rationale as well. On the 15th of April 1944, Gentile was assassinated by Communist terrorists. He is buried in the Church of Santa Croce in Florence—beside the remains of Galileo and Machiavelli.

2

The Background of the Philosophy
of Giovanni Gentile

The philosophical thought of Gentile grew out of a protracted intellectual crisis that beset post-Risorgimento Italy—newly reunited Italy—at the turn of the twentieth century. The nature of that crisis is rarely considered by Anglo-Americans when dealing with Gentile's work and life. Knowing something of the nature of the intellectual and political crisis that tormented Italy at the turn of the twentieth century contributes to our understanding of Gentile's thought. Reading the opening sections of his *Origini e dottrina del fascism* (*Origins and Doctrine of Fascism*), and the first pages of *Che cosa è il fascismo* (*What is Fascism*),[1] one cannot fail to appreciate the deep sense of disappointment that oppressed Gentile when he discussed post-Risorgimento Italy.

For Gentile, Italy's nineteenth-century Risorgimento—its "resurgence," its "renovation," its "redemption"—had failed. The "new Italy," at the beginning of the twentieth century, was not what it could, and should, be. Renaissance Italy had been a magnificence of individual creativity in art and literature—and then it had succumbed to time and circumstance, to decay into the Italy of the late nineteenth century. By that time, Gentile lamented, the Italy of the Risorgimento came to serve as little more than the "easy prey of foreigners, an indifferent factor in a world of hegemonic powers. . . . [It was an Italy] without power, life and reality. . . . The new Italy, formally constituted in 1861, remained . . . more a presumption than a reality."[2]

Post-Risorgimento Italy was conceived, by Gentile and virtually everyone at the end of the nineteenth century, as a nation of negligible

5

consequence in a dynamic world of industrial growth and colonial expansion. At that time, about 18 million Italians lived on doles—on monies transferred to them from Italian emigrant workers living in foreign lands—a humiliating and offensive reality.[3] The nation had little sense of unity and purpose. A flawed assay into African colonialism brought only further humiliation to a government that failed to govern. Millions of Italians had fled the peninsula in order to survive—to labor in the homes, mills, and mines of foreigners—as their servants and manual laborers.

Italian intellectuals responded to all of this with a kind of intensity that found diverse expression in revolutionary velleity, self-deprecation, reactive nationalism, traditionalism, positivism, skepticism, relativism, or idealism—much of it in a confused effort to try to understand Italy's place in the rapidly evolving history of Europe. In the confusion, for example, there were books, written by Italians, themselves, that spoke of the basic inferiority of Latins and the intrinsic superiority of Northern Europeans.[4] The sense of collective failure, humiliation, and inferiority ran deep in the Italian psyche.

Among thinkers, there was an attempt to understand the role of Italian thought in the philosophical processes that accompanied the economic, political, and imperialist development of the major nations of Europe. In the years since the first intimations of industrial development, the thinkers of Northern and Western Europe gave themselves over, more and more, to thought that was largely predicated on the conviction that the purpose of reflection was to make and transform things—to produce.

In England, from Francis Bacon through Thomas Hobbes, one of the central convictions of thinkers was that knowledge should be power. Hobbes held that "the scope of all speculation is the performing of some action, of things to be done." Thought was too difficult, he insisted, for human beings to engage in it solely for the "inward glory and triumph of mind." The purpose of thought was to aid in construction, engineering, architecture, and navigation. It found its purpose in utility, in the doing of things.[5]

Later, for David Hume, intelligence was the maidservant of the survival needs necessitated as a consequence of operating in the world governed by sentiment, belief, and passion. A major thrust of philosophy was to "consider man as chiefly born for action" in a complex and hazardous world—with reasoning supplying a utilitarian guide to behavior.[6]

The acknowledged companion of British empiricism, and utilitarianism, in general, was a notion of science as form of calculation designed to further operations in the world. Similarly, in France, for the Cartesians, thought served to penetrate the mechanics of nature. Out of all this, trends began to separate themselves out of the excitement generated by just such reflections about the natural world.

Materialism made its appearance. In the Germany of the nineteenth century, Ludwig Buechner, Jakob Moleschott, and Karl Vogt conceived the universe as the arena for the operation of determinable and determinate material laws governing all phenomena. The mind, itself, was simply a by-product of the laws of the evolving material universe.

In France, Auguste Comte argued that the world was eminently penetrable, with understanding a function of the recognition of positive empirical laws that governed all things and their development. Darwinism contributed to the process and scientific *positivism*—together with monistic evolutionism—came to dominate the speculation of philosophers like Herbert Spencer, Thomas Huxley, and Ernst Haeckel. For positivism, philosophy came to be understood as nothing other than unified science—its purpose to understand how to discern the discriminable processes that governed nature.

One of the most memorable products of this period was the classical Marxism of Karl Marx and Friedrich Engels. It gave expression to a form of materialism that conceived the universe and human society intelligible only in terms of "scientific" lawlike processes. The development of nature and society followed a pattern of "ineluctable" outcomes—"dialectical and historical materialism"—in which human beings participated as constituent elements in objective and "materialistic" processes over which they had little, if any, conscious control.[7]

In effect, classical Marxism was a form of nineteenth-century positivism. For all its insistence on its "dialectics"—in the forms expressed by its advocates—Marxism was very much like the evolutionary and deterministic positivism entertained by the Comteans, the Spencerians, and the Darwinians. It was fully compatible with the *Weltgeist* of the period. For at least that reason, Marxism was welcomed by many intellectuals in the more industrially advanced nations of Europe and North America during the last decades of the nineteenth century.

During this period in Italy, positivism emerged as one of the most popular philosophical currents. A significant number of intellectuals imagined that it represented the thought of the philosophers of the most advanced industrial nations. Italian thinkers sought to identify themselves with the more progressive communities of the North. By the end of the nineteenth century, positivism, in the form provided by philosophers like Roberto Ardigò and Erminio Troilo,[8] came to dominate Italian thought.

Commencing at least as early as midcentury, Carlo Cattaneo had spoken of the "science of facts" to distinguish "progressive" thought from what he held to be the empty, and purposeless, speculations of philosophical *idealism*—the neo-Kantianism, Thomism, and Hegelianism of nineteenth century Italian philosophy.[9] In the prevailing environment in newly reunited Italy, it was evident that "progressive thought" was identified, almost exclusively, with the systematic rejection of traditional religious beliefs, moral philosophy, and any idealist interpretation of reality.

Italian positivists had committed themselves to the utilitarianism and the scientism of British empiricism and French mechanistic materialism. Cattaneo himself implicitly identified the positivistic posture as essentially designed to serve the exclusive interests of industrial development.[10] Utilitarianism and materialism interpreted the world as typified by mechanical processes, in the sense that development would follow the established patterns of "stages of progress" exemplified in Northern and Western Europe. In all of that, there was extraordinarily little role to be played by the passions, the ideals, the sacrifices or the faith of individuals taken singly or in aggregate.

Most nineteenth-century European thinkers regarded Newtonian physics as an objectively true representation of nature. All the complexity of the world could be somehow reduced to the position and impulse of small, material particles in constant agitation. Given the position and the forces acting on material particles, future developments could be anticipated with the predictability of Laplacean determinism. Society and its changes were no less subject to discriminable laws. In the course of such processes, there was no place for "arbitrary" and willful acts. Whatever ideals were to be discerned among men were the epiphenomenal products of deeper processes taking place in the material foundation of collective life.[11]

By the turn of the twentieth century, however, the Newtonian and Laplacean world vision was to become increasingly subject to qualification. For various reasons, the notion that matter was something that had the property of determinable location in time and space, enormously useful in scientific development since the time of Galileo, was seen as increasingly privative and implausible by the end of the nineteenth century.

In the course of its development, philosophical materialism had led thinkers first to deny the existence of the secondary qualities of matter—and then its primary qualities. Matter was gradually divested of its "objective" "material" properties. Even in his own time, David Hume had allowed that "all the sensible qualities of objects, such as hard, soft, hot, cold, white, black, etc. are merely secondary, and exist not in the objects themselves, but are perceptions of the mind, without any external archetype or model, which they represent. If this be allowed, with regard to secondary qualities, it must also follow, with regard to the supposed primary qualities of extension and solidity . . . "[12]

In fact, by the turn of the twentieth century, experimental physics had almost completely transformed science's notions of matter, space, and time. Traditional materialism could no longer appeal to natural science for support. The wave theory of light, the idea of atomicity, the doctrines of the conservation of energy and of evolution, soon brought forth phenomena that could not be accommodated within the notions of materialism and positivism. As a consequence, various forms of epistemological and ontological idealism became increasingly popular.

"Matter," as a substance, had become increasingly "immaterial." It had become more and more difficult to "objectively" calculate, in nature, both the position and the force of material particles. Scientific prediction came to be understood as less deterministic than probabilistic—involving a direct "interaction" of observers in the process.

In these developments, standard science was to abandon a good deal of its original materialist, and simple empiricistic, biases. The science of Pierre Duhem, Henri Poincaré, Richard Avenarius, and Ernst Mach was conceived of as far removed from the ideal of predictive infallibility so commonly attributed to science during the major part of the nineteenth century.[13]

In the course of these developments, a kind of "anti-intellectualism" emerged that reflected the rising criticism directed against the notion that knowledge could possibly be conceived as a simple product of the mind's "reflection" of externalities. More space was given to the active role of the mind in coming to operate in, and to know something of, the world.[14]

The world of Henri Bergson, for example, was composed not of

simply quantitative elements in measured space and time; it was characterized by a qualitative intensity that was vital and manifestly subjective. While the intellect continued to be understood as a tool of
pragmatic employment, the whole personality of the human being was
seen involved in the creation of something new in the process of
coming to know. Science no longer conceived the world in terms of
simple outcomes of Laplacean determinism.[15]

In the field of social theory, the notion that thought, consciousness,
will, and behavior were the derivative products of primary "material,"
and deterministic, processes became increasingly suspect. That social
developments were "ineluctable" and "inevitable" seemed increasingly
implausible. Increasingly, space was allotted to *consciousness, thought,
will, belief,* and *ethical conviction* in the accounts of social and political development.

In 1897, when he was but twenty-two, Gentile published his "Una
critica del materialismo storico" ("A Critique of Historical Materialism")—his review of classical Marxism as a theory of history.[16] In his
account of Marxism, Gentile reflected on the inadequacy of materialistic determinism as an explanatory device in any explication of social
processes. More and more frequently, consciousness, will, and ethical
imperatives insinuated themselves into any effort to understand social
events.[17]

Gentile's essay reflected intellectual developments in the philosophy of science, epistemology, and social theory that were becoming
increasingly common at the end of the nineteenth century. Fewer and
fewer intellectuals were prepared to accept the thesis that scientific
truth was a function of passive observation. The mind did not simply
"reflect" an "objective" reality; it assisted in its creation. Knowledge
of the world was an interactive process in which the observer, in some
sense, creates reality. In terms of social theory, what this meant was
that the processes that shaped the world of human beings intrinsically
involved human consciousness, volition, and ethical deliberation.

The reactions to all of this, among social theorists, took on a variety
of forms. For some German Marxists, for example, what this meant
was the necessity to supplement the thought of Marx and Engels with
Kantian ethics. For other Marxists, particularly in Russia and Italy,
there was a tendency to introduce increasingly complex psychological
individual and social variables into the making of revolution. For their
part, the more traditional Marxists continued to conceive social theory

as "true" only when it was a "reflection" of prevailing circumstances. With the modalities of the mid-nineteenth century, orthodox Marxists continued to argue that revolution would be the automatic outcome of inevitable (if "dialectical") "material" processes running their course in capitalist society. The result was an "evolutionary socialism" that would emerge when "social and economic trends matured."[18]

By the end of the nineteenth century, Marxists like Eduard Bernstein were prepared to continue to argue that the response of human beings was little other than a function of social reality. Since capitalism had "matured," and had accommodated its proletariat to the *evolutionary* changes that would lead the workers' movement from capitalism to socialism, all the talk of revolution as necessary to bring an end to industrial capitalism was otiose.

In Italy, by the end of the nineteenth century, Marxism had bifurcated into two main trends, an evolutionary Marxism that understood itself to be the consequence of determinate social and economic processes—and a revolutionary Marxism that saw itself a function of the will and determination of a select number of conscious revolutionaries.[19] The first was a Marxism that saw itself the heir of "ineluctable" trends within industrial capitalism itself. The second was the product of French syndicalism, inspired by the voluntarism and moralism of Georges Sorel.[20]

The first accommodated itself to the parliamentarianism of Italian liberalism, and the second advocated revolution *whatever* the social, political, and economic circumstances might be at any given time. In a clear sense, the evolutionary socialism of the first was the embodiment of some form of philosophical positivism; the revolutionary syndicalism of the second, that found its philosophical rationale in the writings of Sorel, was anti-positivistic and increasingly idealistic. Circumstances, economic conditions, and class relations defined the first; will, consciousness, determination, elitism, and ethical considerations characterized the second. Inescapable in all of this was the fact that Italy, at the turn of the century, was a less-developed community, an unfinished nation on the periphery of European industrialization.

In the ferment of the turn of the century, an increasingly assertive collection of revolutionary nationalists, intransigent Marxists, inflexible idealists, and exotic nonconformists made their views known. Philosophical materialism rapidly fell into disfavor.

For practical purposes, one of the foremost objections to traditional (and "dialectical") materialism—as we shall further consider—was the notion that it led to a denial of human responsibility and creativity. In retrospect, the evolving thought of reactive, and developmental nationalists and revolutionary syndicalists—and their anti-positivistic spokesmen—occupy the center of attention.

Giovanni Papini and Giuseppe Prezzolini spoke of a developmental, and "spiritual," nationalism—together with an intransigent revolutionary syndicalism—inspired by a doctrine of voluntarism, elitism, commitment, and sacrifice. Among the spokesmen for both, there was the manifest rejection of any kind of passivity in a world of dynamic change.

Positivism had spoken of an automatic succession of social, political and economic developmental phases. Classical Marxism had intimated that social revolution would be a function of material circumstances—the concentration of capital, the increasing misery of the proletariat, and an irreversible and catastrophic decline in the overall rate of profit in the industrialized democracies. By the first decade of the new century, none of that seemed convincing.

What was sought by reactive nationalists and revolutionary syndicalists was action, a search for heroes, together with functional and moral elites.[21] Anti-positivists of a variety of persuasions made recourse to the thought of pragmatists like William James and F.C.S. Schiller—and that of vitalists and voluntarists, like Bergson and Josiah Royce.[22] Intuitionism, mysticism, theosophy, magism, and futurism all made their appearance in an environment where voluntarism and action were sought—where ideals were the order of the day, where passion and struggle were understood to be the irrepressible necessity for survival in an international environment characterized by a Darwinian struggle for survival.[23]

A tidal wave of journals appeared, *Leonardo, Prose, L'Anima, Rinnovamento, Regno, Ronda,* and *Lacerba,* each of which advocated an anti-positivistic revolutionary *elan*[24]—all part of a revival of religious and secular idealism that became more and more prominent in Italian intellectual life.[25] Life was conceived infused with a passion for development—with an insistent rejection of any passivity and automaticity in the face of internal or external challenge. One can trace the effects of these developments in the thought of the young Benito Mussolini—at that time an intellectual spokesman for Italian Socialism.[26]

In 1904, under the auspices of the International Library of Rationalist Propaganda, Mussolini published "L'Uomo e la divinità" ("Man and the Divinity"), a transcription of a lecture he delivered in Lausanne, Switzerland, to reveal "the absurdity of religion."[27] In the course of his exposition, Mussolini cited, as having supplied the evidence of the nonexistence of God, the "objective methods" of the "experimental science" of Bacon, Galileo, and Descartes. That evidence supported the conviction that the universe was a product of "matter—unique, eternal and indestructible—that never required a first mover nor will ever end." There was little need for the intercession of the "Old Triangle with the white beard." Human beings, themselves, were the complex products of the evolution of matter—and mind was a function of the material brain of *Homo sapiens*.[28]

Immediately after, in the course of the next few years, Mussolini, like a great many others, began to significantly modify his position. Within five years Mussolini was prepared to commit himself to the making of a "new Italy," a "Third Rome," that would be the consequence of revolutionary activity on the part of those Italians who responded to "the new and more profound" developments in the nation's culture. These "new Italians" would reject "Comtean positivism and Spencerian social evolution" for "a philosophy of action, a pragmatic philosophy."[29] More and more frequently, the names of Sorel, William James, Henri Bergson appeared among Mussolini's revolutionary injunctions. He spoke candidly of masses being moved to revolution through the instrumentality of "ideas."[30]

It was during this interval, between a dominant positivism and a rebirth of philosophical activism and idealism, that Gentile assumed his intellectual obligations. Italy was in ferment.

Italy was an economically retrograde and largely ineffectual member of the world community—lacking confidence in itself, divested of purpose, and threatened by those advanced industrialized powers capable of projecting overwhelming power against any nation that resisted their pretenses. It was in that intellectual environment that Gentile came to recognize that part of his obligation was to determine how philosophy might serve the collective interest of an emergent nation that faced the overwhelming external power of imperialism.[31] On the one hand, serious philosophical work would enhance the prestige of the nation; on the other, philosophy would inform the efforts of those responsible for developments on the peninsula.[32] "Little Italy, *Italietta*," so much disdained by the advanced industrial democracies, was in the throes of intellectual, cultural and political revolution.

3

The Philosophy of Giovanni Gentile

It was in that context that Gentile began his intellectual work—and the intensity and drama of that period does much to explain his passion and his intransigence. From the very first, Gentile's work manifested an ardent evangelical quality. It was animated by a clear commitment to the defeat of positivism as a pernicious enemy, the defense of Italy's millennial past, and an unqualified devotion to its future.

For at least those reasons, the work of Gentile seems singularly alien to the thought of most Anglo-Americans. We share little of the psychology of Italy at the turn of the twentieth century—and as a consequence, fail to appreciate what might make Gentilean idealism so attractive to many Italians at that time. Moreover, we tend to be totally unfamiliar with the language—Hegelian and idealist—through which Gentile expressed his technical philosophy.

After the eclipse of the English idealists—such as J. H. Stirling, T. H. Green and F. H. Bradley[1]—the more dynamic trends of Anglo-American thought have occupied themselves with those aspects of philosophy that serve, largely, as ancillaries to empirical science: mathematical logic, theories of probability, semiotics, analytic philosophy, and the philosophy of language. Technology has become so prominent a preoccupation among Anglo-American thinkers—servicing as they do the needs of a fully industrialized and rapidly developing post-industrial economy—that humanistics has become almost unintelligible.

To most immediately service the needs of technology, many Anglo-American thinkers have simply followed "common sense," and conceive the world as a place external and independent of the individual

15

and of collective consciousness, composed of mind-independent things and peopled by empirical persons, each of whom is acquainted with that external world through five senses.[2] The consequence has been the steady decline, among Anglo-Americans, of interest in "speculative idealism" and "metaphysics."

Most Anglo-American thinkers, of course, recognize that any notion of an external world composed of ultimate ontological constituents that might be conceived of as mind-independent, massy, impenetrable particles, would be hopelessly anachronistic. With the isolation of the electron at the close of the nineteenth century, ontological atomic materialism began to make less and less sense. With the advent of quantum physics in the twentieth century, it became generally recognized that human beings are made aware of the presence of "ultimate particles in nature" *only* when the particles are disturbed by minute electrical interchanges with some other part of the universe. These exchanges force the atom to indicate a position, and a quantity of heat. What the atom is, before those disturbances, is quite impossible to say.[3] All the qualities of the atom of modern physics are derived; it has no immediate and direct physical properties at all; all are observed through the disturbances we create in interacting with the submicroscopic world.

It becomes quite meaningless, in those circumstances, to ask what the ultimate constituents of the world might be independent of our experience of them. We succeed in symbolizing their activity in an abstract multidimensional space by partial differential equations. For physicists to speculate on the "essence" of atoms is a futile occupation.[4] Most contemporary thinkers consider the atom to be like the square root of minus one in mathematics. Although elementary mathematics maintains that among ordinary numbers no such square root exists, the introduction of the new symbol simplified the most important mathematical propositions. *Its use is justified by that convenience.* Similarly, physics illustrates that atoms cannot exist as simple objects—but their introduction makes possible a coherent formulation of regularities governing physical and chemical processes. The criterion for the admissibility of a concept is not whether it "truly reflects objective reality" but rather whether it leads to a simpler and more useful characterization of phenomena.[5]

For thinkers caught up in the flood of technical changes that typify modern industrial and post-industrial development, all of that is simply taken in stride. Utility, efficiency, and production are the dominant concerns. The concerns of epistemological idealists like Gentile lie elsewhere.

While Gentile maintained an abiding interest in science, as such, he was more directly concerned with the totality of experience in a world largely dominated by abstractions. He, himself, labored to understand not science alone, but the entire "human experience." He occupied himself with what he called the "humanistic conception of the world."[6]

He sought to understand how human beings came to fathom their world. How they might, beginning with raw experience, construct a "reality" so dense and complicated that only few could feel comfortable within it. In his search, he commenced with raw experience, the immediate awareness of the "self," the "mind," or the "spirit" as something interacting with a mind-independent "objective world."

For Gentile, to begin one's speculation about the world with "pure human experience" means, at least, that the entire analysis would turn on the nature and the properties of *consciousness*—not consciousness as it is understood in empirical psychology, but consciousness understood as philosophical *mind*, or *spirit*, in the tradition of German and Hegelian idealism.

Gentile sought to credibly account for the complex intellectual products that allowed his contemporaries to begin to put together a philosophically coherent picture of human experience. More than that, he sought to provide his co-nationals with a conception of things that might permit them to meet the challenges of the early twentieth century. To understand Gentile's philosophy is to understand something significant about the rise and appeal of Italian Fascism in its time.

Given such a contention, it is curious that there are so few systematic treatments of the thought of Gentile in English.[7] He is almost entirely unknown among Anglo-American intellectuals. That is unfortunate, because, as has been suggested,[8] his association with Fascism renders his thought of significant historical and ideological interest.

Before the advent of Fascism, Gentile's thought was of acknowledged interest and importance to some Anglo-Americans.[9] Within the Italian philosophical tradition, it had earned a place for its integrity and congruity.

Between 1912 and 1916, Gentile had laid down the principal outlines of his Actualism—his neo-Hegelian interpretation of human experience.[10] For our purposes, his first statement, *L'Atto del pensare come atto puro* (*The Act of Thinking as Pure Act*),[11] delivered in nineteen tightly written paragraphs, is of marginal utility. The entire discussion is synoptically written and necessarily requires explication. For the purposes of exposition, the volume of 1916, *Teoria generale dello spirito come atto puro* (*The General Theory of Mind as Pure Act*),[13] on the other hand, provides more ready access to his thought.

In the exposition of his Actualism in 1916, Gentile begins with references to the English empiricist tradition—a tradition familiar to Anglo-Americans. His first reference is to George Berkeley and Berkeley's account of "ordinary" human experience.[14] That account was the product of a critical assessment of John Locke's notions of what might constitute human understanding.

For his part, Locke sought to provide human beings with a reasonable comprehension of what they need to know in order to believe only what they ought to believe. In the course of his inquiry, what he thought to be a rational interpretation of sense experience emerged.

As an empiricist, Locke's world was composed of material objects—and the minds in which those objects were "reflected." Like most contemporary Anglo-Americans, he was a commonsense "realist." He understood "objects" as existing in a qualifiedly mind-independent external world. Subsequent British thinkers, George Berkeley, for example, found emphatic difficulties with his notions.

Gentile reminded us that for Berkeley, Locke's "concept of material, corporeal, extended, substance, of bodies existing outside the mind was self-contradictory, since we can only speak of things which are perceived, and in being perceived things are objects of consciousness—ideas."[15] Under that interpretation, the "real world" of Lockean commonsense realism immediately becomes indefensible. Its reality could only be warranted exclusively by "perceptions," "impressions," and "sensations"—all inextricably part of the furniture of the finite, empirical mind. To argue, as Locke seemed to do, that a mind-independent "real-world" of matter was "reflected" in the mind was very problematic. The only things we had as evidence of such a real world would be *perceptions*—that were *mind-dependent*. It was not evident how one might credibly move from mind-dependent perceptions to evidence of a *mind-independent* "objective world."

Berkeley, of course, rejected any notion of a mind-independent material world. The "material world," for him, was a fiction. He argued that *being*, the existence of the "external material world," could only be perceived, and hence, confirmed through sensory evidence. As a consequence, Berkeley reminded his audiences, "To be is to be perceived." If that were the case, one was compelled to maintain, in some sense, that the "external world" was mind-dependent.

For Gentile, Berkeley's reasoning was impeccable. Berkeley erred only when he argued that those objects that naive realists take to be the real world—all "perception-constituted"—are caused by the direct spiritual intervention of God, who is "ontologically perception-transcendent." Gentile maintained that if human beings could not argue from perceptions to the "objective" existence of a mind-independent external material world—they could hardly argue from their finite perceptions to the existence of an infinite and perfect mind-independent deity. Berkeley's God was presumably mind-independent and perception transcendent. Any notion of a "spiritual reality" outside human consciousness and beyond perceptions was as indefensible as the "commonsense" conviction that there was a "material world" similarly beyond and independent of human perception.

For Gentile, Berkeley was an inconsistent idealist—in effect, a "realistic intellectual." If Berkeley's thesis was that "to be is to be perceived"—that the world is epistemologically and presumably ontologically mind-dependent—it would be hard to sustain belief in the existence of a divinity that was mind-independent—that could not, under any conceivable circumstances, be perceived.[16]

Hume's objections to Berkeley are in part rooted in the same inconsistency pointed out by Gentile. Hume attempted to return to a conception of reality that was once again grounded in direct perceptions, and indirectly confirmed by intersubjectively established experience. Gentile, for his part, maintained that the problems that attended Hume's effort were no less difficult to resolve than those intrinsic to the thought of Berkeley.

Hume argued that the external, mind-independent world becomes known to us only after our custom—and habit-influenced faculty of imagination has worked on the impressions of sensation. Only then do sensory impressions take on the character of being an experience of "external objects." Hume began with sensory impressions—and only with the intercession of the mind, memory, and the relations among ideas—did the mind put together some features of the world and other persons. In effect, for Hume, at the very beginning of the human enterprise, "the mind has never anything present to it but . . . perceptions, and cannot reach any experience of their connection with objects."[17]

Granted all that, Hume went on to argue that "mixed mathematics," the studied formulae of mind-generated, non-empirical "relations of ideas," could somehow be projected over the mind-independent external world. As a consequence of all that, Hume suggested that thinking human beings might thereby come to some doubtful knowledge about a mind-independent "natural world."

For Gentile, all that simply pointed to the fact that while the realist presupposition of a knowable, mind-independent, external world is an important fiction for natural scientists,[18] its merits are entirely, and exclusively, *utilitarian*. Epistemologically, the notion of a mind-independent, external world, cannot be demonstrated. "Naive realism, scientific realism, philosophical realism," Gentile maintained, "irrespective of all the pretenses of its most obdurate defenders, is invariably very ingenuous, because it can be easily seen that whatever is found [in the so-called "external, objective world"] is either invented or constructed by thought, and can be nothing other than thought."[19]

Gentile held that "for the modern scientist, natural or mathematical science is not imagined to be a representation of [an indepenent] reality, but a . . . construction fashioned by the spirit."[20] "Reality" is not an independent object with which thinking must somehow contend. "Reality" is inextricably *immanent* in thought and thinking; it is a product of thought. "Nothing," for Gentile, "transcends thought. Thought is absolute immanence."[21] For Gentile, only "the concept of mind," and nothing else, could be "unconditional reality."[22]

Thought, *pensiero pensato*, and thinking, *pensiero pensante*, constitute the *immediately* confirmable, ultimate reality of the world.[23] For Gentile, the only epistemologically consistent, and philosophically defensible idealism was an *absolute* idealism—an idealism that integrated all things conceivable within its scope and range—within a mind, a consciousness, a spirit, without limits.[24] Gentile held that only an idealism that presupposed nothing, and was prepared to argue that nature, history, art, religion, politics, society, and economics were all to be embraced, penetrated and resolved into the "act of thinking" could be true. His convictions, in effect, were "totalitarian" in essence.[25]

However we structure conscious experience, whatever criteria we accept as evidentiary grounds for the truth status of our individual claims, our knowledge of the world is, according to Actualism, inextricably mind-dependent. All of its complexities, its analytic elements, its concepts, its demonstrations, its regularities and law-like affirmations, its proofs, confirmations, and controlled replications are the consequences of simple and compounded *choice*, acts of implicit or explicit *will*.[26]

For Gentile, knowledge of ourselves and of the world was never the product of passive observation. All knowledge is the product of a conscious *choice* on the part of active consciousness for which we individually and collectively were *responsible*. His was a conception of knowledge predicated on the *voluntaristic doctrine of the truth*.[27] In the torrent of impressions, perceptions, or "percepts," we choose among them, we relate them, organize them, fashion them into processes— and select among such constructs *those that work—those that contribute to the realization of individual or collective purpose*.[28] In that sense, Actualism displayed some features of generic pragmatism and the humanism of F. C. S. Schiller.[29] Knowledge, even in its *abstract* form, as particular science, was, at least in one significant sense, necessarily *useful*. It guided human activity as a functional instrumentality. It was a truth that was "a part or an aspect of the truth."[30] It was a truth that was the product of abstractly considering the *subject* as *consciousness*, as distinct and separate from "external reality" as *object*.[31]

Abstract or particular science was understood to be "a relative negation of the subject . . . with the object . . . produced by the . . . elaboration of scientific thought . . . dealt with as 'naturalistic.'"[32] Science, for Gentile, was systematized "common sense." Received thought (*pensiero pensato*) provided an essential part of the "elaboration" to which he refers. But that thought, as "natural," is "abstract," "unreal." "Concrete" logic involves the concreteness of philosophy. It is presuppositionless.

The received thought of mathematical or natural science is integrated into living thought (*pensiero pensante*) by virtue of a process that involves logic, definition, classification, typologizing, and confirmation—all standardized as the "scientific method"—the elaborate collaboration of thinking subjects immanent in universal thought. Gentile's emphasis is not with the processes that are familiar as standard science, but with the intrinsic nature of the "concrete logic" that "unites" the abstract objects of science with the active subject of philosophy.[33]

The purpose is to reveal to human beings that "life in its fullness is neither art, nor religion, nor science. It is morality."[34] Concrete thought exemplifies not art, or religion or science, but morality, and by necessity, liberty.[35] Actualism, as a general theory of spirit, presents itself as a system of life.

It cannot be our purpose here to pursue Gentile's thought through the intricacies of its entire development and exposition. For our account, it is enough to recognize that "the nucleus of Gentile's entire speculative system resides in his identification of reality with thinking in the concrete process of its *self-realization*."[36]

Self-realization, for Gentile, was the fundamental *moral imperative* of human beings. In his final work, *Genesi e struttura della società* (*Genesis and Structure of Society*), he maintained that "philosophy is continual vigilance and reflection over what we are, and what we make of ourselves. . . . That dialectic of self-consciousness . . . is the root of philosophy."[37] He maintained that in his *Sistema di logica* (*System of Logic*),[38] he had shown that there could only be a single absolute category in actual, concrete thought that was both universal and free—the thinking self—in which the entire life of a conceivable universe is resolved into the spirit—the thinking subject.

Gentile argued that only as spirit might human beings comprehend the moral character of life. For Gentile, "whatever *is* is nothing; it becomes something by becoming spirit, self-consciousness. . . . The whole creation of the universe is here in the self-creation of the spirit."[39]

For Gentile, thinking is the matrix out of which all things emerge. In a concrete act of thinking, the human being fashions both his universe and himself. For that reason, the human imperative is *self-actualization* (*sii uomo!*) through *thinking*.[40]

What is absolutely clear is that for Gentile, systematic thought—philosophy—is an intensely moral enterprise. It is the process through which the human being fashions himself or herself. And in that process, the "objective" universe is fashioned as well.

Gentile thus argued that the most elementary epistemological considerations teach us the fundamentals of life. The notion that the individual was born into a fixed and finished world—there to labor within the strict confines of a mind-independent reality—could only be an elaborate and stultifying fiction.[41]

Whatever we know of experience indicates that the mind gradually fashions "reality" out of the raw materials of "sensations." The creation of an "objective reality" is a long and complex process that is forever ongoing and ever-changing. Within that process, both the individual and the world change. The true and concrete subject of that entire process is not the "empirical individual" that is thrust into the world, but the "transcendental ego"—that spiritual reality in which the "empirical ego," and all "particular" things, find their ultimate unity.[42]

Everyone is prepared to acknowledge that the "reality" of primitives and children is something far different than the reality of cultivated adults. Even the concept of the "self" is different in various cultures. The differences are a function, over time, of the complex spiritual activity of thinking as both particular and universal.[43]

There clearly are any number of problems that attend Actualist notions. For our purposes here, at least two are important: the first is the possibility that such an actual idealism collapses into *solipsism*— that all of being should resolve itself into one's *personal consciousness*.[44] If experience is conceived to be nothing other than the experience of the individual—each of us, at best, would be a "windowless monad," creating and inhabiting his own subjective world.[45] There could be no morality, for each of us could not reasonably be expected to do anything other than pursue his or her selfish interests. There could be no real knowledge, since all knowledge would be *subjective*. Without special argument, one could not meaningfully distinguish between subjective and intersubjective knowledge claims—there could hardly be grounds for distinguishing cognitive error from truth. Under such circumstances, one could never be said to make, or have made, cognitively informed moral choice. Solipsism would be the defeat of Actualism. Conscious of that, Gentile clearly rejected solipsism, as well as the relativism and the moral anarchism that attended it.

For Gentile, solipsism was a *morally indefensible* position. In thinking, he argued, we define ourselves against an "external world," something *conceptually* other than ourselves. The somethings of that external world are "outside" ourselves—and while those somethings are in spirit, they are not of spirit. As objects of consciousness, some are other than consciousness; they are external "things." But *persons* cannot simply be things. They *behave* differently than things. They interact *spiritually* with us, making claims on our attention, affection, commitment, and sacrifice. Solipsism is a practical absurdity.[46]

Other selves display *spirituality*. They initiate spiritual activity. With them, we share spiritual fellowship. With them, and their fellowship, comes immediate apprehension, an understanding of "the other." With a fellow being we share "a deeper unity" than we share with things.

In effect, in the world in which we find ourselves, "we want more than intellectual unity. . . . The abstract activity we call mind no longer contents us, we want the good spiritual disposition, what we call heart—good will, charity, sympathy, open-mindedness, warmth of affection."[47] As was the case in the works of Friedrich Schelling and Josiah Royce—for Gentile the existence of other selves was understood to be a *moral necessity.*[48] It was necessary if human beings were to be ethical creatures.

For Gentile, modern philosophy was necessarily concerned with the moral problems faced by contemporary human beings. As a response, "modern philosophy, as pure idealism," he argued, was compelled to be "essentially [a system] of ethics."[49]

In his final work, Gentile held that "the human individual is not an atom. Immanent in the concept of an individual is the concept of society. For there is no ego, no real individual, who does not have with*in* him . . . an *alter* who is his essential *socius*—that is to say, an object that is not a mere 'thing' opposed to him as subject, but a subject like himself."[50]

For Gentile, the reformed Hegelianism that informed his system required an intrinsic source of development, the immanent opposition of A and-A. It involves an epistemic "dialectical logic" familiar to students of German Idealism.[51] For our purposes here, the progressive unfolding of the "self-consciousness of the self" means that the "empirical ego," the empirical self, requires a corresponding "non-ego" if it is to achieve all the qualities of personhood.[52] The "true object" of the developing subject is "a partner; for in order to be *ours*, the object must cease to be a thing and become another self; or, more exactly, *the* other self, our own alter ego, the partner within us who joins with us in the society that is innate in the transcendental Ego, and which may therefore be fairly styled *transcendental society.*"[53]

All of this, of course, can be expressed without Hegelian language. Providing synoptic expression of the more formal delivery characteristic of Gentile's work simply provides the occasion to indicate that there was nothing solipsistic or irrational in his views. The translation of his thought into social and political injunctions entails recourse to neither "evil" nor "irrationality."

As shall be argued, as early as 1919, Gentile had insisted that individuals were not moral atoms, they were social creatures who realized their truest selves in social communion. He rejected any notion of a social reality that involved isolated selves, coming together fortuitously, innately possessed of "inalienable rights" and irrepressible individual interests.[54]

For Gentile, the conception of the empirical individual intrinsically implied the conception of society—a system of rules, the embodiment of voluntary choices, that governed the behaviors of moral equals.[55] It was inconceivable to him that thinking persons could imagine that individuals could subsist outside of society. Without a society of equals, within a system of laws, the individual, for Gentile, was inconceivable.

The second problem that critics regularly mount against Gentile turns on the appearance of *mysticism* that seems to characterize Actualism.[56] In mysticism—the argument proceeds—all distinctions are lost. There is an intuition or immediate apprehension of some "supreme reality as one, eternal and indivisible."[57] Finite particular things, including our specific personalities, disappear into the "womb of the featureless infinite"—to disable human effort, discourage scientific research and impair the pursuit of rational understanding.[58]

Gentile dealt extensively with mystic thought, and he did acknowledge that the charge of mysticism had been directed against his entire system. For Gentile, *myth* was a form in which religion represented its truth—a kind of truth that appeals to no distinctions in time, place, category, or multiplicity.[59] The differences between mysticism and the idealism of his system, he insisted, turned on the fact that, "idealism reconciles all distinctions, but does not, like mysticism, cancel them, and it affirms the finite no less resolutely than it affirms the infinite, difference no less than identity."[60]

As has been suggested, Gentile held that science—as distinct from his philosophy of the spirit—distinguished itself by its *abstract* qualities.[61] Science posits the existence of a "real" world in extension, mind-independent, and characterized by mensurable properties. In that context, empirical scientists study categories of particular "external objects." "Every science," Gentile argued, "is one among others and is therefore particular. . . . A naturalistic view is the basis . . . of every science. Thence the logically necessary tendency of science in every period towards mechanism and materialism."[62]

Human beings tend to intuitively conceive experience in terms of mutually exclusive subjects and objects—thinking selves as opposed to a given mind-independent externality[63]—even though contemporary thinkers recognize that the "reality" to which the schemata of science apply are products of the thought of scientists themselves. "Natural or mathematical science," Gentile reminded his readers, "for the modern scientists, is no longer conceived a representation of an [external] reality, but as . . . a construction that the spirit makes of its object."[64] Today, almost every thinking person is prepared to concede that the reality with which the science of numbers deals, for example, is a function of mathematics itself—a "reality that constructs itself out of the same thought that recognizes it." Modern empirical scientists concede that the theoretical frameworks by virtue of which they come to know "objective" nature, are modifiable schemata they themselves fashion.[65] Empirical science, as we all acknowledge, is in a constant state of flux; "objective" nature is forever changing. The nature and properties of atoms, subatomic particles—the dimensions of space, the character of time[66]—are all in constant alteration.

Within that context, Gentile does not reject the particular sciences; they are understood to have their own integrity. They provide the features and the determinate being without which universal thinking would be devoid of character and substance. Thought, the ground of all that is "thinkable," is "infinite autodistinction." The content of universal thinking (thinking as "pure act") manifests itself through the "abstract logic" we recognize as empirical science—as particular truth claims supported by particular methods of verification.[67]

Gentile argued that none of this constitutes a threat to the integrity or independence of the several sciences. What it does is to direct attention to those problems, legitimately philosophical, with which most applied scientists do not concern themselves.[68]

For Gentile, there remain those problems—that do not generally occupy applied or theoretical scientists—concerning the relationship of empirical inquiry to the thinking self. Gentile finds the notion of a "real" world, external to the thinking self, an insupportable epistemological presupposition. However useful to the empirical scientist, the conviction that we find ourselves in a preexistent world—the nature of which we simply discover—threatens to dilute its *moral* quality.

If there is a prefabricated external world into which we are thrust at birth, most of our responsibilities are unacknowledged and are progressively diminished. Our freedom, *ab initio*, is restricted. We imagine ourselves the products of genes and the environment, functions of complexes and familial trauma, inextricably dependent on external contingencies.

Gentile argued that if we understand ourselves in terms of living thought, sharing with other selves the illimitability of thought—and through communion making decisions based on shared concepts of validity and verifiability—we freely create an "objective world" for which we are *ultimately* fully responsible.[69] He fully understood that most human beings simply accept the world as it is presented by "common sense" and authority. He acknowledged that only few persons would exercise the intellectual freedoms implicit in a moral universe. None of that dissuaded him from his account.

Gentile attempted to offer an alternative to the notion that there was an external, "scientific" and mind-independent world that controlled our freedom to choose. For Gentile, the life of the spirit was intrinsically unconstrained. "Everywhere we find only the self-creative activity of the spirit: art, religion, science, economics, philosophy, everything arises from this self-constitution"—ultimately, the products of human choice.[70]

By thinking, we labor to solve problems. We can simply accept the solution of others to those problems, or we can attempt our own assessments, controlled by our purposes, and how effectively we hope to operate in any given environment. Since our self-constitution of the world necessarily implies that we are responsible for the world we accept, "there is no corner of the earth, no moment of the day in which man can escape from the imperious voice of duty. . . . Within the soul of man there is a still small voice that is never silent, and will not let him rest, but spurs him ever onward. Onward toward what? Toward himself—toward the ideal self that he ought to be."[71]

In effect, there was very little mysticism in the thought of Gentile. His Actualism provided place for mysticism and myth within the compass of thinking, but it also provided the distinctions without which empirical science could not survive. Gentile's Actualism was no threat to science. Science was an integral part of his inflexible and all-consuming moral conception of life. Science, for Gentile, was a particular affirmation of man's creativity, part of humankind's responsibility for creating ideal human beings who seek the ultimate fullness of self.

For Gentile, the entire process of coming to know the world inextricably involved human beings in a universe of free, willed moral activity. That activity is free because there is no demonstrable externality to which thought must conform.[72] The thinking subject, given his purposes, chooses what is to be real. It is thus willed, because the activity is free. It is moral, because the activity of the thinking subject is selectively chosen with respect to given ends.[73]

Within the context of this complex moral philosophy, with its epistemological and metaphysical supports, there is no place for either solipsism or scientific obscurantism.[74] Gentile's views were anti-positivistic, not because he objected to empirical science, but because he understood positivism and scientism to be predicated on the metaphysical notion that a "natural world" existed independent of mind—a thesis that he found epistemologically indefensible.[75] More than that, he saw any form of ontological realism, involving a conviction that human beings could only come to know the world by observing it as spectators, to prescind from their direct, active, and moral involvement. The passivity and non-involvement implicit in this notion he identified with a characteristic disease of reason: "intellectualism."[76]

For Gentile, intellectualism was neither epistemologically defensible nor morally tolerable—denying as it did, implicitly and explicitly, volition, action, and morality. For Gentile, intellectualism was a form of impaired reason.

4

Gentile's Political Philosophy

As early as the advent of the First World War, Gentile had drawn implications from his technical philosophy that applied to politics. Long before the advent of organized Fascism, he had written extensively on issues that engaged Italy's domestic and international political interests. By the end of the Great War, Gentile had made his political views eminently clear. In the nationalist journal, *Politica*, he made public a fairly complex conception of politics.[1]

Gentile maintained that Actualism, as an activist conception of life, was deeply "preoccupied with the concrete problems . . . that must be confronted and resolved." In terms of solving problems, Gentile distinguished his political thought from that of those who imagined that individuals faced a preexistent political and social reality, with respect to which they could only passively adapt. Gentile argued that Actualism conceived the reality in which individuals operated not as something external to, but as a product of, consciousness—the product of a series of willed collective moral choices. Given such a conception, in order to address the most urgent problems that afflicted retrograde Italy at the turn of the century, Gentile argued that the nation must consciously create for itself an international "personality that would be valued in the world." Italy had too long been the "prey of strangers."

To accomplish its purposes, Italians would have to give themselves over to a sense of selfless mission—a sense that they were responsible for the world in which they chose to live. That sense would inform the collective will. The consciousness of mission would generate the energy and moral commitment on the part of the community necessary for the accomplishment of its historic tasks—all of which Gentile saw as implied in the Actualist conception of human responsibility.[2]

29

Italy demanded the
inst. existence of
a strong state
representing
the moral
personality
of the
community

Gentile argued that the circumstances in which Italy found itself demanded the institutional existence of a strong state, itself representing the moral personality of the community. "The State[3] [is to be] conceived as a moral reality, a substance that realizes itself through the free and ethical will" of its citizens, expressed in a "faith," in what Gentile identified as a "religious conception of life."[4]

Gentile's entire political philosophy was characterized by a conception of collective life that understood individuals to be fused together in an immanence (a "transcendental self") that manifests itself in a continuity of culture, economics, politics, and history—a shared transcendental consciousness. Empirical individuals were but transient distinctions within an inclusive transcendental political reality. They found their moral fulfillment only in the state that embodied that reality. The "ethical state" was a transcendental agency—"deeply rooted in the history and the national consciousness . . . , a solid foundation in political, social, economic and spiritual reality."[5] The ethical state was the linchpin of Gentile's political philosophy.

That state was not to be imagined as *inter homines*, as something contractually contrived by individuals, but rather as *interiore homine*, as something intrinsic to human life. Human beings, for Actualism, possessed an essentially social essence. The liberal notion that individuals could exist anterior to society was dismissed as a puerile fiction.[6] The state, as the effective moral sense of the community, was intrinsic to the very conception of a human being. As the vehicle of the sense of collective responsibility, the state enjoys a philosophical and ethical priority with respect to the individual. It has an organic continuity that transcends the life of individuals—and, as such, makes meaningful the life of each. It supplies the historic elements that shape personality, lend substance to cognitive assessment, and inform moral choice.

Gentile conceived nationality, in our time, to be the major formative factor in the evolution of human personality. At different historic periods, the family, or religion, constituted the foundation of the social consciousness of individuals. In the modern era, it is the nation that is the foundation of ethical choice, uniting everyone in the state as the one sovereign institution in and through which the individual continually fashions and refashions himself. Any political conception that imagined the state to be a "sum of the interests of individuals or of particular interests" would be not only fundamentally mistaken, but irremediably immoral as well. It would fail to perceive the "concrete," "transcendental" individual in the "abstract" individual of common sense.

In a world characterized by the reality of intense international competition, a catalog of demands makes claim on the individual. Within that reality, the individual must fashion circumstances in which he can fulfill himself—and which will provide the same opportunities for his progeny and his co-nationals. Where individuals have been corrupted by a protracted period of philosophical individualism and its attendant egotism, they must be made aware that true self-fulfillment cannot be attained without identification "with the universal"—without becoming one, through the state, with the historic community. Such an identification demands a total commitment, making the individual "party to an iron discipline, united in the realization of a transcendental moral reality." In the modern world, if the nation is to prevail, the state must take the "amorphous material" left it as a consequence of the influence of liberalism, and shape it into a "unitary and free" community—a "political organism that would acquire a vigorous historic concreteness," capable of realizing its potential and that of its citizens.[7] That could only be accomplished when the multiplicity of individuals is fused in infrangible unity—when the individual identifies with the state as a transcendental self.

The consciousness of identification with the community on the part of individuals is largely a pedagogical product. Individuals are educated to the awareness of their moral responsibilities. For that reason the state—the state which undertakes that education—cannot be "agnostic." It must superintend the education of its people. If the ethical state, for Gentile, was religious in character, it was also pedagogical in terms of its primary responsibilities.[8]

For the leadership of the state to allow the education of individuals to be subject to an anarchy of irresponsible influences emanating from special interests, would be morally remiss. Individuals would never escape "particularity." For liberals to argue that such an environment, open to any and all biases, egotisms, stupidities, and perversions, provided an open "market place of ideas" makes a mockery of responsible intellectual exchange.

During the Fascist period, Fascists were to echo the same argument and consistently maintain that individuals in parliamentary democracies were inundated with suborned influences, serving occult interests and personal profit, inimical to a coherent appreciation of collective interests.[9] They were to maintain that in such circumstances not only were individuals morally debauched, cognitively unfree, but that the entire environment was intellectually and morally debased.

The political leadership of an ethical state—the effective elite, or a notable individual—represents forces in action in any given context. Popular consciousness, in turn, reflects some measure of the historic significance of those forces. Any elite, or any leader, who represents those forces and that collective consciousness, embodies the will of the community. The passive or active acceptance of that leadership represents consent. If education is corrupted, the popular will becomes uncertain, and the state is bereft of legitimacy and continuity.

At its historic best, a political leadership invokes faith, selfless ideals, sacrifice, and an abiding sense of mission among a people: "A people is in fact a people in so far as it feels itself a people—and it feels itself a people in the fantasy of its poets and in the memories and the hopes of its writers, but most of all in an effective will that expresses its significance to the world." That effective will and that significance becomes manifest only in the activities of the state—and those activities become reality in the behaviors of the man or men "who represent the tendencies already apparent in a people, the already operant forces. . . . having a solid foundation in political reality." Only "by virtue of this common consciousness [expressed through an effective State] . . . does a people become a concrete and dynamic actuality."[10] Without it, the collectivity lapses into moral torpor—and is overwhelmed by others and by events.

By the end of the First World War, Gentile had decided that the times required a fundamental change in the moral consciousness of Italians if they were to overcome the afflictions that rendered Italy of negligible account in the modern world. A sense of renewal must be invoked, to be animated by "new ideas and a new spirit." There must be "a substantial interior transformation capable of redirecting and disciplining all the energies that the Great War had revealed, in order to make Italy capable of a vast productive undertaking, social pacification, and reorganization of the State."[11]

With the making of the "new men" requisite for Italy's future, the individual who imagined himself possessed of an independent reality, endowed with irreducible selfhood and inalienable rights, comes to realize that true liberty and freedom are only possible within the "love and faith" that reveals itself in a commitment to the community. There is a recognition that the moral realization of ourselves can only be a function of our collective identity with the ethical state.[12] Individual freedom and personal fulfillment are functions of identification with a free and ethical state.[13]

Gentile dismissed the notion that the state could be the simple mathematical product of bargaining between individuals and special interests. He identified that entire notion as an immoral fiction that limited the empirical individual to a reprehensible egoism that would leave him unfulfilled, a shadow of what he might be.[14] Liberalism, carried to its ultimate conclusion, would leave the individual a denizen of an antinomian society—a member of a debased aggregate in which one felt responsible to neither moral nor public law.[15]

Thus, by the end of the Great War, Gentile had drawn out the political implications of his philosophy. He early associated himself with the nationalism of the Associazione nazionalista of Enrico Corridoni and Alfredo Rocco—both later to figure prominently in the Fascist regime.

Without identifying himself with what he considered their "materialism," he nonetheless found sufficient similarities between their views and his own to write for their publications with some regularity. Both the nationalism of the Associazione and Actualism were anti-individualistic, antiliberal and antiparliamentarian. The nationalists of the Associazione were statists by conviction, and developmental in intention.[16] They, like Gentile, aspired to the moral renovation and rehabilitation of Italians, the palingenesis of the nation, and resistance to the impostures of the "plutocracies" of the modern world.[17]

In all of this, the prefigurations of Fascism are clearly visible. Still uncertain in 1919, very soon Fascism took on all the philosophical and political trappings of a special form of nationalism—that found in the works of Gentile. By that time, Gentile's works were among the best known in Italy. In his pedagogical writings, he anticipated the state's role in the creation of a willed consensus that gave overt expression to the "transcendental society" implicit in any and every human being. The state embodied that transcendental essence that ensured the viability and the moral substance of the national community.

There is every indication that Mussolini's invitation to Gentile to join his government immediately after the March on Rome was anything but casual. Gentile's Actualism offered the prospect of a doctrinal unity that might accommodate all the disparate forces that originally contributed to the success of Fascism. Already in August 1921, Mussolini had written to Michele Bianchi that Fascism required "a body of doctrine" if it were not to self-destruct.[18] As will be argued, after 1921, Fascism sought a coherent doctrinal incorporation of the views of all the elements that had fallen behind its guidons. By 1925, that process had been all but concluded with the adoption of Actualism as the philosophy of Fascism.

Actualism would show itself to be capable of providing doctrinal coherence to all those active forces operative within the Fascism that had emerged from the war. Not only had Mussolini himself made the transition from the positivism of orthodox socialism to idealism, but the most radical Marxists of prewar Italy had followed the same trajectory. By the time of the First World War, many of those calling for Italy's involvement were already antipositivists—activists, pragmatists, futurists, voluntarists, elitists, and idealists—all of which attested to a rapidly emerging intellectual synthesis.

By the end of the Great War, the outlines of Gentile's political convictions were apparent—and widely broadcast. More than that, Gentile had demonstrated his ability to effectively address the intellectual weaknesses of Fascism's most intransigent opponent: orthodox Marxism. As early as the turn of the century, Gentile had already advanced a more damaging assessment of classical Marxism than had Benedetto Croce. By 1920, Gentile had become at least as important in Italian intellectual circles as Croce—and he offered a more penetrating critique of the thought of Marx and Engels. He offered the prospect of an intellectual victory for Fascism against a system that pretended to doctrinal superiority. While still a student, Gentile had already undertaken a penetrating assessment of the early work of Karl Marx as philosophy and as a theory of history.

5

Gentile and Marxism

Giovanni Gentile displayed an interest in the thought of Karl Marx as early as 1897 when, as a twenty-two year old, he published his essay, "Una critica del materialismo storico" ("A Critique of Historical Materialism"). Two years later, he published "La filosofia di Marx" ("The Philosophy of Marx"). The latter essay, written more than a century ago, reveals Gentile's substantial knowledge of the thought of Marx—and demonstrates the relevance of an emerging Actualism to the subsequent articulation of his political philosophy.[1]

More than that, Gentile's discussion of Marx's philosophy and "theory of history" reveals intellectual affinities between Gentile and Marx not readily acknowledged by contemporary thinkers, generally loathe to find any significant relationship between the thought of Italian Fascists and Marxists.[2] In that context, it is of some significance that both Fascist and Marxist thought traced their origins to the idealism of Hegel—that of Gentile through the intermediate revisions (among others) of Bertrando Spaventa—and that of Marx through the neo-Hegelian formulations of Ludwig Feuerbach.[3]

Gentile's essay on the philosophy of Marx, cited by V. I. Lenin as a significant work,[4] argues that the youthful Marx was anything but a standard epistemological and ontological *materialist*. In retrospect, it seems transparent that the epistemological and ontological position assumed by the young Marx was something other than it was to subsequently become in the writings of Friedrich Engels or Lenin.[5]

To make his point, Gentile undertook an analysis of Marx's gloss on the first of the "Theses on Feuerbach," written by the founder of "historical materialism" in 1845.[6] In its substantial entirety, the first thesis reads:

The chief defect of all hitherto existing materialism (that of Feuerbach included) is that the thing, reality, sensuousness, is conceived only in the form of the *object* or *of contemplation*, but not as *sensuous human activity*, *practice*, not subjectively. Hence, in contradistinction to materialism, the *active* side was developed abstractly by idealism—which, of course, does not know real, sensuous activity as such. Feuerbach wants sensuous objects, really distinct from the thought objects, but he does not conceive human activity itself as *objective* activity.

The meaning of the gloss is not immediately evident, but it provides Gentile with sufficient material to make his case. Gentile contends that the point of Marx's objection to "all hitherto existing materialism" is essentially that advanced by every post-Kantian idealist, i.e., that materialism conceives the object, the "external world" as a datum, as something "given" to experience—something simply contemplated, rather than something that is a product of the interaction of the subject and the object.[7]

One of the principal contentions of Actualism, as we have seen, was that if a mind-independent "reality" was conceived as composed of objects extrinsic to the subject—things simply contemplated—there would be no credible way to confirm any correspondence between them and the "sensory impressions" they presumably caused.[8] That is to say, if we entertain only "images" in the mind—"impressions" presumably received from an external world—there could be no way to certify the accuracy, the correspondence, of such impressions with the external world—for we can never stand outside the presumed relationship and compare the "image," the "impression," with the "real world" conceived to be its cause.

Idealism, in general, contended that knowledge could only arise out of an *intrinsic* and *active* relationship between subject and object. Idealists argued that laypersons, possessed of the conceptual apparatus of "common sense," conceived of an abstract object, "reality," appearing to an abstract subject, the empirical self. It is only the unspoken presuppositions entertained by common sense that allow the process of coming to know the external world to appear at all feasible. The fact is, it is actually the synthesis of "reality" and "self" in *consciousness* that constitutes the ground of "concrete" and confirmable knowledge. Somehow or other, the object and the subject must be "intrinsic" to each other.

In his *Economic and Philosophic Manuscripts of 1844*, the young Marx outlines a remarkably similar epistemological assessment. There, he argues that "consciousness knows the . . . object . . . because it knows the object as its *self-alienation* [*Selbstentaeusserung*]."[9] The object is to be understood not as something simply sensed, but must rather be understood as something somehow intrinsic to the subject, as a "self-alienation," or, as Marx explains the thesis: "knowing knows that in relating itself to an object it is only *outside* itself—that it only externalizes itself; that *it itself appears* to itself only *as an object*—or that which appears to it as an object is only it itself."[10]

While these manuscripts were unknown to Gentile when he wrote his essay on the philosophy of Marx (being made available only in the mid-1930s), the epistemological posture was so familiar to him that he could reconstruct it from his analysis of Marx's gloss on the first thesis on Feuerbach. Gentile recognized that Marx's expression "activity through objects (*gegenstaendliche Taetigkeit*)," was to be understood as implying that "sensuous activity" could somehow "fashion, posit, create the object."[11]

In 1844, Marx had spoken of "real, corporeal man, man with his feet firmly on the solid ground, man exhaling and inhaling all the forces of nature," positing "his real, objective *essential powers* as alien. . . . *Human* objects are not natural objects as they immediately present themselves, and neither is *human sense* as it immediately *is*—as it is objectively—*human* sensibility, human objectivity. Neither nature objectively nor nature subjectively is directly given in a form adequate to the *human* being." "Here," he went on, "we see how consistent naturalism or humanism is distinct from both idealism and materialism, and constitutes at the same time the unifying truth of both."[12]

At that point, Marx's epistemology displayed features that were essentially idealistic—certainly it was not remotely akin to the materialist notions of knowledge common in that time. The difference, of course, between the epistemology of the young Marx and that of Gentile, turns on the fact that Marx understood the motive energy of the creative activity of the knowing subject to emanate not from the needs of *spirit* or *consciousness*, but from the essential *natural* needs of the human agent.[13]

In his "corporeal," "material" needs, the human agent embarks upon "sensuous activity." In that activity, the human being defines himself as subject against those objects meeting his needs.[14] Sensuous activity is the process through which subject and object are distinguished for what Gentile identified as the "empirical," and Marx characterized as the "natural," individual.

For Marx—as was the case for Gentile—the individual does not *passively* reflect the object in sensation; he or she *actively* develops a consciousness of an intrinsic relationship with it. For what is the subject without the object? and the object without the subject? Subject and object are correlative terms, the one inevitably carrying the other in its train.[15] The object that arises out of what Marx identifies as "human sensuous activity" can be said, in some sense, to have been "created" by that activity; and since there can be no object without a corresponding subject, it is necessary to add that in "creating" the object, the subject "creates" him-, or her-, self.[16] The object is, as Marx insists, a "self-alienation" of the subject, a *Selbstentfremdung*, an alienation of self in other.[17]

In effect, according to Gentile, the young Marx was a "dialectical" materialist—a materialist attempting to press a singularly idealistic form over a "naturalistic" content. In retrospect, it seems reasonably clear that as a student of philosophy, Marx sought to resolve the epistemological problems that German idealism had inherited from British empiricism.[18] In his attempt, Marx dismissed the notion that sensations were simple passive responses to external, mind-independent "reality." That much he had learned from German idealism.

At the same time, he accepted the materialist presupposition of Feuerbach's reform of the Hegelian dialectic. Life concerned itself not with the activity of *ideas* or *consciousness*, but with *material* "reality."

Thus, whatever else he was, Marx was an ontological realist, having accepted Feuerbach's proposed materialist reform of the Hegelian dialectic. Feuerbach had maintained that "the beginning of philosophy is not God, not the Absolute, not Being as a predicate of the Absolute or the Idea—the beginning of philosophy is the finite, the determined, the real."[19]

The materialism of Marx was thus presumptively "realist"—but a realism characterized by a number of peculiar properties. It was a realism that somehow understood coming to know the "real world" as an activity involving interaction between the "ego and the non-ego." His "naturalism" or "humanism" sought to preserve some of the essential features of the Hegelianism out of which it emerged—while substituting a self-subsistent, external, and material world for the *spirit* and *consciousness* of epistemic and ontological idealism. For all that, matter would somehow be invested with some of the properties of spirit. The unity of the ego and the non-ego, the "sensuous activity" in which the world and the self would unite, looked suspiciously like the union of the object and the spirit characteristic of the idealism of Hegel and Gentile.

It is very clear that Gentile held such a philosophical half-way house to be intellectually untenable. A materialistic mimicry of the Hegelian dialectic could not be long sustained.[20] It was clear that, in the short or long term, Gentile expected at least two negative developments: (1) he suggested that such an epistemology, given its intrinsically unstable character, could only rapidly decay into a simplistic epistemological materialism[21]; and (2) that Marxism, in all of its variants, because of the implications of its materialism, would inevitably fail to sustain any serious moral intent—committing itself to some form of determinism that would preclude any possibility of significant human choice in the course of human affairs.[22]

Marxism, from its very commencement, according to Gentile, was afflicted with the major disabilities of what he identified as "philosophical realism." For one thing, the world was dogmatically conceived of as mind-independent. For another, it was held that knowledge concerning that mind-independent external reality was delivered through the senses.[23] Finally, realism carried the implication that the external world was entirely indifferent to human purpose, and that its laws deterministically governed the individual and collective life of humankind.[24]

However arguable Gentile's claims may be, they are supported by the main features of Marxism as it matured. When, in later years, Engels chose to assume the obligations of developing some sort of epistemology for "dialectical materialism," it became evident that he chose some form of realist representationalism to serve his purpose—a kind of "picture theory" of reality—rather than attempt to apply the notions of the young Marx to his problems.[25]

Unlike the young Marx, Engels was prepared to argue that human beings, in interacting with a mind-independent world, received, in mind, "reflections," or "images" of "external" material objects. Such reflection (*Wiederspiegelung*) was understood to be a mental copy or picture (*Abbild, Abklatsch*) of an "external" and "objective" reality.[26]

How images or representations might be understood to "reflect" the external world has always been a problem for representationalist epistemologists. At best, representationalists use terms like "reflections" and "pictures" metaphorically. No one can sensibly argue that we receive "pictures" of external objects in consciousness via our sensory organs. Engels certainly could not mean to imply that the relationship between the mind-independent, external world, and a consciousness that perceived it, could be captured in the expression "copy" or "picture." Rather, he seems to argue that there is some sort of "correspondence" between them.[27]

As has been suggested, the problems generated by this kind of "representationalist or correspondence theory," is familiar to epistemologists. Engels tried to argue for such a correspondence by suggesting that since consciousness is a product of the human brain, and both the brain and the external world are products of nature, they must somehow "correspond."[28] Such an argument can be sustained only if an indeterminate number of suppositions are accepted.

One missing premise of this kind of argument is that since everything is a product of natural evolution, survival requirements assure that man's consciousness is going to be a suitable tool for navigating through a dangerous universe. Hence, consciousness must provide us accurate "reflections" of reality.[29] When we successfully succeed in negotiating our environment, we confirm the accuracy of our "copies," "reflections," and "pictures." That argument looks suspiciously like it assumes what it is obliged to prove.

In effect, Engels leaves us with an epistemological *pragmatism*, having very little to do with the sophisticated *dialectical* epistemology left us by the young Marx. The position Engels assumes is manifestly unconvincing as a serious epistemology. What he argues is a commonplace—that, as human beings, we are capable of *surviving* in the world—not that we have come, thereby, to *know* it. The mind-independent, external, material world that is postulated by pragmatists of Engels' stamp could be composed, equally well, of unknowable things-in-themselves—and we might still be able to successfully pick our way among them without *knowing* them in any real sense.

Following this line of flawed argument, Lenin insisted that not only was the material world fully independent of our consciousness, but that it was *fully cognizable* through the agencies of the human senses.[30] There have been few materialist philosophers heroic enough to hold such a view. Hobbes, for example, spoke only of sense perceptions delivering "phantasms," "representations," and "appearances" of a presumed mind-independent external world.[31] The relationship between "appearance" and external reality was *causal*, not representational. He did not pretend to know what the "world-in-itself," independent of human consciousness, might be.

In the nineteenth century, Helmholtz described the relationship between sensory impressions and the "objective properties" of the external world by stating that the "perceived differences (i.e., color) are the appearances [*Erscheinungen*] of given objective differences in the qualities of the external bodies. . . . Sensations are therefore the naturally given sensory signs [*Zeichen*] or symbols for objective qualities."[32] Whatever correspondence he conceived between perceptions and the world was certainly not captured in the notion of a sensory "picture" of reality.

For most materialist epistemologists, sensations serve, in some sense, as "appearances," or "symbols" of mind-independent, external properties. The relationship between sensations and external properties was uncertain. Sensations were understood to be "signals," "correlates," or "signs" of certain properties of externally existing reality—not their "copies," or "pictures."

In the writings of the young Marx there was no suggestion of such a view. Marxist epistemology, over the years, had simply decayed into the representationalism of the later Engels. He tried his hand at formulating a suitable epistemology—to be followed more relentlessly by Lenin—only to leave serious epistemologists perplexed. For Marxists and Marxist-Leninists, the result was cognitive decay.

Lenin could only observe that "Engels speaks neither of symbols nor of hieroglyphs, but of copies, photographs, images, mirror-reflections of [external] things. . . . If sensations are not images of things, but only signs or symbols, which do 'not resemble' them, then [the] initial materialist premise is undermined."[33] All of which is very curious indeed.

Throughout the twentieth century, Marxists of every variety have attempted to deal intelligently with such epistemic problems. That they would prove so difficult was first suggested by the young Gentile.[34] Ultimately, Soviet Marxists came to accept the privative notion that sensations were "pictures" in mind that somehow "resembled" mind-independent external objects and their "real" properties. While prepared to consider Marx's views, Gentile had summarily dismissed any and all such forms of representational realism.[35]

In fact, the Soviet Marxists of the twentieth century had remarkably little success in making sense of any of these issues.[36] Given the evident inability of sensations to tell us very much about the nature of a mind-independent "objective world," Lenin—in the final analysis—resigned himself to the fact that the "philosophy of materialism" did not have to assign *any* qualities to that world. He finally reduced his argument to the claim that "the *sole* 'property' of matter with whose recognition philosophical materialism is bound up is the property of being an objective reality, of existing outside our mind"[37]—a singularly uninformative notion fully compatible with at least objective idealism or epistemological skepticism.

In substance, Marxist-Leninist epistemologists have never felt obliged to tell us anything about the mind-independent "natural world" that presumably gives rise to sensations. All they had to dogmatically affirm was its "existence" outside "our" mind.

Some Marxists realized the intellectually indefensible position of such an interpretation of the relationship of consciousness to an external mind-transcendent reality. Max Adler simply rejected the entire assessment. He said, "The acceptance of a reality independent of our consciousness . . .and knowledge of it . . . is sheer metaphysics . . . because [such notions] transcend experience. Whether such a reality is conceived as matter or spirit, it is in any case something not given in experience, and in no way subject to empirical confirmation."[38]

In his exposition, almost half a century before, Gentile had made the same case. He argued that Marx had never been a materialist in the sense that Engels had been a materialist. He consistently argued that Marx had been a materialist *metaphysician*—a convinced neo-Hegelian—something very different.[39]

Gentile argued that Marx saw the "objective" world in terms of self-developing, teleological activity—in terms of a world having an end, a goal—having all the properties of the Hegelian spirit.[40] Marx's notion of the "real world," Gentile argued, was something vastly different from the real world of nineteenth century empirical science. Empirical science, Gentile reminded us, provides, at its best, *tendency* statements—not ineluctabilities. Marx's affirmations about the world, the world of capitalism, were framed not as tendency statements, but as *logical entailments*. Marx's work was not intended to serve heuristic, mnemonic, didactic or experimental purpose—the purposes of scientific speculation and research[41]—but was addressed to imagined futures, to utopias long awaited and sorely sought. Marx, for Gentile, was a *metaphysician*, in the traditional, and in his specific, meaning of the term.[42]

Engels, in fact, had attempted to fully formulate such a metaphysics—left incomplete by the young Marx. To that purpose, Engels held that "both matter and its mode of existence, motion, are uncreatable [and indestructible] and . . . therefore, their own final cause." Thus we have a notion of a universe composed of matter and motion—indestructible, infinite in space, and uncreated in time—that serve as their own cause.[43] According to Engels, all of this moves inexorably toward the creation of thinking man and to his final goal—the end of history. "Matter" ceases to be a scientific category, that is, subject to empirical confirmation or disconfirmation, and becomes a *metaphysical principle* harboring both teleological and moral purpose.[44]

Neither Engels nor Lenin ever succeeded in seriously addressing any of this to anyone's real satisfaction.[45] For their part, many non-regime Marxists addressed those concerns with varying degrees of success. What is clear is that Gentile anticipated many of the issues that were to perplex Marxists, Marxist-Leninists, and their critics. In fact, the clutch of problems that surrounded Marxist and Marxist-Leninist epistemological concerns was only one set of issues that Gentile anticipated.

If epistemological and ontological questions were matters of relative political indifference, Gentile alluded to more important issues to be joined in dealing with Marxism as a theory of history. He maintained that materialists—whether "mechanical" or "dialectical"—were compelled, by their principles, to abandon any notion of a world that has within it a place for moral considerations that engage human will and decision.

For Gentile, ontological realists inevitably find their moral concerns crowded out by the properties of the external world they postulate. In a materialistic construction of the world, Gentile argued, human beings become increasingly subject to the mind-independent laws of matter. Genetic and environmental determinants are increasingly postulated as governing the behavior of individuals, and the behaviors of aggregates of individuals. Ultimately, the individual, or the collective, no longer enjoys any freedom to make choices. Soon, there is no longer any place for choice, for morality or ethics, in a life governed by externalities.[46]

Gentile argued that such would inevitably be the case for Marxism in any of its variants. In retrospect, it certainly appears to have been true in the case of the dialectical materialism of Marxism-Leninism.

When Marx wrote his most enduring essays, he was prepared to argue that human behaviors and human interaction were the "ineluctable," "inevitable," and "determinate" consequence of the manner "in which men produce their means of subsistence." What individuals are, according to Marx's account, "coincides with their production, both with *what* they produce and *how* they produce. The nature of individuals thus depends on the material conditions determining their production."[47] The form of intercourse between individuals is *determined* by production; the "division of labor *determines* also the relations of individuals to one another."[48]

All of that, together, determines "the production of ideas, of conceptions, of consciousness," which is "directly interwoven with the material activity and the material intercourse of men." On the basis of "their real life processes," Marx insisted, "the phantoms formed in the human brain are also, necessarily, sublimates of their material life process. . . . Morality, religion, metaphysics, all the rest of ideology and their corresponding forms of consciousness, thus no longer retain the semblance of independence. . . . Life is not determined by consciousness, but consciousness by life."[49]

By the time of *The Communist Manifesto*, Marx could argue that the revolution he anticipated was "inevitable"—the product of empirical "social laws."[50] Equally clear was the conviction that "forms of consciousness, religion, philosophy, ethics, etc. etc. . . . trace their origins and growth from. . . . the real process of [material] production."[51] Gentile had been correct. For Marxists, as materialists, morals and ethics could only be by-products of social and natural laws. They were epiphenomena of determinate and discriminable natural processes. Humankind was caught up in natural laws that determined individual and social behavior. Morality and ethics were, in the last analysis, functions of economic development.[52] Human behavior was determined by the empirical laws of social and, ultimately, economic development.[53]

Throughout the years, Marxists of all sorts have attempted to attenuate the determinism that characterized the Marxism of Marx and Engels, by suggesting that the economic substructure of society did not *determine*, but rather "profoundly colored," "conditioned," "influenced," and "affected deeply" the moral and ethical behaviors of individuals and aggregates of individuals.[54] The efforts have never really been convincing. The entire notion that individuals, and groups of individuals, were morally responsible for their conduct was hopelessly impaired.

The young Gentile seems to have been right concerning what he considered Marxism to be and what he expected Marxism to become. In terms of its major variants, the philosophical materialism of Marx and Engels resulted in determinism and amoralism.

In dealing with the issue, Lenin was candid. He stated, "One therefore cannot deny the justice of [the] remark that 'in Marxism itself there is not a grain of ethics from beginning to end'; theoretically it subordinates the 'ethical standpoint' to the 'principle of causality'; in practice it reduces it to the class struggle."[55] Gentile had suggested no less.

Throughout the history of Marxist-Leninist movements, Marxist-Leninists have attempted to deal, intellectually, with the issue of the role of ethics in society and in terms of individual conduct.[56] They have not been notably successful here any more than they have been successful in dealing with the epistemological questions inherited from the young Marx and the less capable Engels.

Lenin left his heirs with the simple assertion that "our morality is entirely subordinated to the interests of the class struggle of the proletariat. Our morality is deduced from the class interests of the proletariat."[57] Morals and ethics were predicated on class struggle—with one class favored because social evolution was moving "inexorably" in the direction of the proletarian revolution that would bring with it "equality," "fraternity," "abundance," "freedom," and the total lifting of "exploitation."

Given the world-view they had inherited, Marxist-Leninists knew that morality could only reflect "the objective laws of social evolution." Morality was nothing other than the product of "a consistent determinism." Morals, and its rationale in ethics, were understood to be the simple reflection of social evolution that inextricably involved "class struggle." Given the entire rationale that saw world history governed by a teleology leading to a communist society, anything that furthered the success of the proletariat in that struggle, however bestial, was moral and ethical.[58] "Good" was understood to be anything that furthered the victory of the proletariat over the bourgeoisie.[59]

Given all that, together with the conviction that only the Communist Party possessed the "true science" of social evolution—being the sole agency equipped with infallible truth concerning the course of human history—the Party was understood to be "the conscience of the people," to be exclusively charged with the "deep moral responsibility for the future of the people and its homeland," as well as the education of the anticipated "new socialist man."[60]

For Gentile, all of this was to be expected. Marxism, and Marxism-Leninism were seen as a peculiar form of positivism—the scientism that characterized the nineteenth century. For Gentile, all ontological realists were condemned to follow similar paths. What was unique was that Marxists so singularly misunderstood the rationale that they advanced as legitimation for their rule, that they did not appreciate its true character.

Gentile held that Marxism, in all its variants, was a metaphysics—having little to do with the falsifiable propositions of empirical science. Marxism, for Gentile, was a "degenerate"[61] and self-contradictory neo-Hegelian idealism that pretended to be a materialism that displayed the major properties of spirit. Marxism's descriptions of the "dialectical materialist" world reflected the properties of idealism out of which it emerged. Marxism's world was a world informed by teleological processes, that had goals and purposes. While it was a world filled with moral intent, the individuals in it had little if any moral choices. It was a world that required human activity, but offered little latitude for human will and human decision. It was a world designed to deliver cognitive, sentimental, and emotional fulfillment to human beings in which human beings, per se, played curiously negligible roles.

For Gentile, all these concerns were to occupy him throughout his life. They were to influence the articulation of his social and political philosophy. His study of the early Marx left a clear residue in his subsequent reflections.[62] Years later, when he was preparing those manuscripts from his youth for publication, he did not hesitate to remark that he felt himself moved. He recognized among those pages some ideas that he still retained—and which contributed to the formulation of a new philosophy of the emergent Italy he sought.[63] It was that philosophy that he was to enlist in the service of Fascism.

6

Gentile and Fascism

From his earliest youth Gentile gave expression to a passionate patriotism. As a young man, he lamented the fatherland's defeat at Adua in 1896—in newly reunited Italy's first assay into colonial conquest. He early learned to deplore the passivity and the indecisiveness of Italians. It was not long before he sought the making and remaking of Italians as standard-bearers of a newly reunited nation no longer ready to submit to the duplicity of foreigners. He was humiliated by the disdain with which Italy was treated by the more industrialized nations of Europe, and longed for a "Greater Italy"—when the nation, once again, would be an actor on the world scene.[1]

All of that fueled his antipositivism. He was convinced that positivism was an intellectual and moral disability that impaired the judgment and the character of his co-nationals. That conviction made of him an antisocialist, opposed as he was to the positivism of orthodox Marxism. He sought some device that might make Italians active moral agents, committed to the creation of a renovated and redeemed nation. Like the idealists with whom he identified himself, Gentile acknowledged that the Italian nation was only then, at the end of the nineteenth century, recreating itself out of the remnants left by centuries of oppression and exploitation at the hands of foreigners.[2]

Several things emerged out of his early nationalism. Gentile recognized that in order to make Italy great, it would be necessary to remake Italians—a philosophical and pedagogical enterprise of consuming magnitude. It was an enterprise that would involve investing Italians with an intransigent *faith*, an obdurate *commitment*, and an inflexible *will*, capable of sustaining profound *self-sacrifice*, unremitting

47

labor, and military *discipline*. To that end, Gentile charged himself with the responsibility of formulating a philosophy of life suitable for human beings burdened by history with a demanding mission.

To that purpose, he gathered around himself a number of intellectually aggressive pedagogical activists who sought massive reforms in the educational system of the peninsula.[3] By the time of the First World War, Gentile's nationalism had fully matured. He was loosely affiliated with the Nationalist Association of Enrico Corradini, and collaborated with Alfredo Rocco in the publication of the nationalist journal, *Politica*. Corradini was to go on to become a major political figure in the Fascist regime, and Rocco was to become a major Fascist theoretician—literally the architect of the Fascist state.[4]

At a time when Mussolini was first abandoning the positivism of his early youth,[5] Gentile had already put together the militant idealism that was to inform his political philosophy. He had already associated himself with *La Voce*—the journal of Giuseppe Prezzolini—that was to have "fundamental and decisive" influence on the subsequent intellectual development of Mussolini.[6]

Years later, Gentile was able to affirm with conviction that he had not discovered "Fascist ideas" after the March on Rome. He had been a "precursor" of Fascism years before its advent.[7] All of that is more or less reasonably well known among those who are familiar with the intellectual history of Fascism. What will be attempted here will be something more than a simple acknowledgement of the affinities he shared with Fascism. It will be a schematic account of Gentile's personal contribution to the articulation of Fascist doctrine.

What will be argued here will be that Gentile provided Fascism some of its most fundamental elements—elements without which Fascism, as a body of thought, would have lost much of its identity, integrity, and persuasiveness. In order to make the case, it is necessary to reconstruct some portions of the social and political thought of Gentile that are particularly relevant. Initially, that takes us back to Gentile's earliest writings on Karl Marx and Marxism.

When Gentile wrote his essays on Marx's philosophy, he dealt with one issue that was to become central to his political philosophy—and to that of Fascism. That issue was his identification of humans as "communal beings." In his last Fascist apologetic,[8] Gentile identified his conception of human beings as intrinsically "communal"—creatures that are, in essence, social and political—as the core of his social

[handwritten margin note: humans as communal being]

philosophy. Within that conception, the individual was understood as one whose "universal" or "transcendental" aspect was the state—a notion that made the liberty of the state the liberty of the individual.

Gentile identified the rudiments of a very similar conviction in the early writings of Marx. In dealing with Marx as a neo-Hegelian, Gentile immediately recognized that Marx was ill-disposed to treat human beings as *particular* individuals. "According to Marx," Gentile argued, "the individual as such is not real; only the social individual is real. . . . The individual outside society and history is an abstraction. . . . The essence of man . . . cannot be determined other than as a species, . . . determined by the totality of social relations."[9]

Thus, in the sixth thesis on Feuerbach, Gentile reported that Marx had written, "the human essence is no abstraction inherent in each single individual. In its reality it is the ensemble of . . . social relations." The reality of man was not to be found in his abstract individuality, but in his *concrete* "transcendental" community. Man, for Marx, was in essence not an individual, but a "communal being"—an assessment that was an unmistakable Hegelian inheritance.[10]

For our purposes, the importance of that particular intellectual conviction can hardly be over-emphasized. What it produced was a disposition, on the part of Marx, to dismiss the emphasis on individual rights that characterized "bourgeois democracy" since the time of the American and French revolutions at the end of the eighteenth century. In documents that were perhaps unknown to Gentile, Marx drew out all the implications that Gentile had intuited from the "Theses on Feuerbach." For Marx, given his treatment of the individual as "unreal," the "so-called rights of man" constituted no more than a defense of "egoistic man," the "individual withdrawn into himself, into the confines of his private interests and private caprice, and separated from the community"[11]—what Gentile called "abstract" individuality.

Given the set of convictions Gentile had identified as central to Marx's social philosophy, in his "On the Jewish Question," Marx had argued that the historic bourgeoisie dealt with human beings only as private individuals, putting particular "egoism and selfish need in the place of . . . species ties," to, in the end, "dissolve the human world into a world of atomistic individuals who are inimically opposed to one another."[12] Marx saw the reality of individuals, not in their particularity, but in their concrete "species being."

Marx argued that what "bourgeois rights," and "bourgeois democracy" produced was the creation of egoistic individuals, shorn of community, who find themselves "oppressed" and "confined" by their own society and their own political state. Conceiving himself restricted by the community and the political state in his effort to obtain "liberty" and "happiness," the individual struggles against the community and the state for "liberation." In such political circumstances, Marx argued, "the sole bond holding [individuals] together is natural necessity, need and private interests, the preservation of their property and their egoistic selves." In any attempt to satisfy any other need, the individual finds himself everywhere obstructed by society and the state. As a result, the human being is reduced to "a partial being" rather than a natural "communal being"—a circumstance which denies his "essence" and leaves him fundamentally unfulfilled.[13]

In substance, given his sense of the communal nature of man, Marx understood bourgeois democracy to be a system suffering a fundamental inadequacy. However expansive the political rights it might deliver, such a democracy must necessarily leave man, as a "species-being," devoid of "real" human freedom, reduced to a "partial being." The "bourgeois state," Marx maintained, could never be anything other than a "framework external to individuals, as a restriction of their . . . independence."[14]

As long as the bourgeoisie failed to deal with human beings as "species-beings," whatever political arrangements were contrived could only be unsatisfactory. As distinct from "partial beings," "communal beings" were persons who lived in a society in which each was understood to be one with his "other"—in which egoism had no place—and the effortless identification of members of the community was a fulfillment of the "essence" of each.

Later Marxists were to package these concepts with content, making material and political equality principal components of community. But more than that, the implications of such a posture is that there is a "natural" and fundamental compatibility between the interests of the individual and those of the community. Marx and Engels had both argued that the interests of the individual worker, the proletariat, and humanity, in some ultimate sense, were one and the same. The individual proletariat was his class writ small. Only those who did not recognize "the objective laws of social evolution" failed to recognize that.[15] They would allow individual egoism to obstruct the seamless unity of the socialist community.

Failing to understood all that, "bourgeois" democrats would seek to institutionalize political "rights" and "freedoms" in society as though the individual and organized society were antagonists—and the rights and freedoms of the solitary individual had to be protected against the pretenses of the community. Because no real freedom was forthcoming for man, as a species-being, fictive freedoms would have to be supplied to man as a "partial-being."

Gentile was to carry essentially those same arguments into Fascism. How important they were to become will shortly become evident. Throughout its tenure, the Fascist argument against "bourgeois or liberal democracy" was sustained by the same logic that Gentile isolated in the early writings of Karl Marx. It was an Hegelian inheritance—shared both by Marxism and Fascism—and it was to shape the political history of the twentieth century.

Years before the advent of Fascism to power in Italy, Gentile gave expression to his reflections concerning the relationships among the individual, society, and the state. For Gentile, the "bourgeois state," the revolutionary state of the American and French revolutions, was a state predicated on the "opposition of the individual to the state. . . . [with] the state conceived as external to the individual . . . in his abstract particularity, outside the immanent ethical community."[16]

Gentile identified this conception of the relationship between the individual and the community as a product of "Spencerian pseudophilosophy" that "opposed the individual to the state . . . seeing the collectivity as the mere sum of individuals" abstractly considered.[17] For Gentile, democratic liberals never understood that "the state is not *inter homines*, between individuals, as it might appear. It is *in interiore homine*—it is intrinsic to the individual—immanent in the consciousness of the citizen."[18] The real individual was not the abstract, empirical individual, but the concrete, spiritual being whose transcendental essence was communal. For Gentile, the community, and its form as the state, was the universal aspect of the individual—they could only be opposed when each was considered in abstraction.

Gentile maintained throughout his life, beginning in the first years of the 1920s, that the *true* individual was a *communal, social*, being. To imagine themselves each to be "one individual among others, a particular, finite, unit" would render human beings incapable of fulfillment. "There is no one possessed of an active intelligence," Gentile maintained, "who would not rebel against a political and social atomism of this kind, which fragments and suppresses the substantial unity of human community."[19] Such social atomism "refuses to acknowledge the ethical substance and the effectual reality of the State as that community, . . . the living root of [man's] very personality."[20]

In order to achieve the fullness of self, the human being must think. As a "thinking being," the human being cannot be conceived to be "the single, particular person." For the solitary individual, without the community of selves, thinking would be impossible, for there could be no language, no confirmed truths, no coherent memories for the solitary individual. As such a "particular" being, the human being would be bereft of speech, and of reason, itself. Such a being "would be less than he could be, should be, and wishes to be." In "speaking, acting, and reasoning," the individual leaves the isolated, particular self behind—and only thus does he transcend barriers to unite with others—others who constitute his larger, transcendental self."[21]

Not only is the "conception of the individual as a social atom . . . a pure fiction. . . . but there is no such thing as a human individual who is really human and really is an individual, who does not recognize a given society as *his* society" and a given state *his* state. The real individual, and not the abstraction of liberal political thought, is he who finds among others a "community of human feeling. . . . For at the root of the 'I' there is a 'We.' The community to which an individual belongs is the very foundation of his spiritual being. It speaks through his mouth, feels with his heart, and thinks with his brain."[22] Gentile consistently held that the state is the will of the community, the universal aspect of the individual.

For Gentile, the concept of human beings as "communal" creatures always remained central to his moral and political doctrine. The moral injunction to fully realize oneself, *"sii uomo,"*[23] could be achieved only in community—within the state. For Actualism, the community was conceived to be the true reality of the individual. In a significant moral sense, the community was understood to be prior to the individual—for outside the community there could be nothing that might pass as an individual.[24]

The entire conception of man as a "communal being," shared by both Marxists and Fascists, sharply distinguished the political doctrines of both from that of political liberalism. Liberals conceived humankind in terms of individuals—and society and the state as the product of their contractual coming together. Among liberals, moral *[handwritten margin notes: "Liberals choose, → moral pirous other compromise between personal interest & artificiality (of community)"]*

choice could only be a compromise between personal interests and those of the artificial, contractual community. The pursuit of egoistic self-fulfillment invariably involved tension with the larger community. The state was almost always understood to serve as a magistrate, a mediator, an intermediary in the conflicts between "free men" and the community in which they lived.[25]

That both Marxists and Fascists conceived human beings as essentially "communal," was given significantly different theoretical expression by the theoreticians of each persuasion. For Marxists, whatever the qualifications subsequently made, there was a conviction that any sense of communality was the product of "material life conditions." Thus, Marx could argue, "does it require deep intuition to comprehend that man's ideas, views and conceptions, in one word, man's consciousness, changes with every change in the conditions of his material existence, in his social relations and in his social life? What else does the history of ideas prove, than that intellectual production changes its character in proportion as material production is changed?"[26]

The material life conditions of the bourgeoisie created a fragmented and schismatic consciousness different, and opposed to, that of the proletariat. The entire logic of the argument turned on the conviction that group consciousness was a function of society's economic base. Marx mocked the notion that "ideas" could survive without the material conditions out of which they arose. The "will" of French socialism, he argued, "presupposed the existence of modern bourgeois society, with its corresponding economic conditions of existence." He ridiculed the entire notion that "historical action" would "yield to the personal inventive action" of intellectuals and political leaders.[27] Engels, in turn, simply affirmed that "revolutions are not made deliberately and arbitrarily, but that everywhere and at all times they have been the necessary outcome of circumstances entirely independent of the will and the leadership of particular parties and entire classes."[28]

As materialists, Marx and Engels conceived human consciousness and will to be the epiphenomenal products of material life conditions.[29] For Fascists, as idealists, the causal order was reversed. The sense of community, the direction of will, the generation of faith, the sense of duty, the intransigence of discipline, the surrender of self, were all conceived products of moral choice, education, personal integrity, and voluntary commitment—"the essential conditions of moral and political character."[30]

For Gentile, the communal sense that informs every human being is the overt expression of a consciousness that is not personal—of a consciousness that very early senses the moral and cognitive need of others in a community of family life, language, art, religion, and science—a felt need in terms of sentiment, rules, intuition, shared aesthetic criteria, and standards of truth.[31] Human beings cannot be conceived as asocial beings. They are indisputably communal creatures united in spiritual communion.

For Gentile, it was not material life conditions that produced the community as the essence of man; it was the spirituality of humanity itself that found expression in community. For Marxists, community was a function of class identity. For Gentile, community was a function of history and culture in the nation.

These notions of man as a communal being make up the philosophical core of Actualism. For Gentile, the reality of human beings was in their moral and cognitive consciousness—a consciousness that increasingly revealed itself, as individuals matured,[32] as impersonal and communal—and ultimately universal. That consciousness was conceived as a limitless and ever-changing spirituality, shared with the living and the dead, in which each person finds and fulfills himself.[33]

Gentile had given expression to all this years before the first Fascists came together in March 1919. During the years between the turn of the twentieth century and the end of the First World War, the men who were to become the intellectual and political leaders of Fascism had undergone major changes in theoretical perspective and philosophical allegiance.[34]

As has been suggested, by the first decade of the twentieth century, Mussolini, himself, had rejected the positivism that had dominated Italian intellectual life for almost the entire latter half of the nineteenth century. Before the end of the first decade of the twentieth century, Mussolini was convinced that positivism, with its objective law-like determinism, and perfectly predictable historic change, had rendered moral outrage, sacrifice, commitment and duty irrelevant—and made revolutionary commitment superfluous.[35] Given the "truths" of positivism, incitements to revolution could only be futile gestures. Mussolini understood positivism to have "banished will and violence from the world [together with] revolution."[36]

Given all that, Mussolini was to soon argue that "positivism, with its evolutionism, had become a trifle antiquated. Those of us who are young," he went on, "breath a different atmosphere."[37]

An entire wing of the Italian socialist movement had assumed something of the same position. Under the influence of Georges Sorel, and the vitalist thought of Henri Bergson, some of Italy's most radical Marxists moved into the ranks of revolutionary syndicalism—in which will and moral conviction became critical concerns.[38] It was during that period that Mussolini probably first came under the influence of Gentile's Actualism.[39]

What should be recognized at this point is the fact that Mussolini, whatever else he was, was a collectivist, who conceived human beings as social animals.[40] He had learned that man was a communal being from Marx.

Around the time that he identified himself with revolutionary syndicalism,[41] Mussolini became familiar with Giuseppe Prezzolini's *La Voce*, a journal that characterized itself as "militantly idealist"—at first giving expression to a form of idealism that was inspired by Benedetto Croce only to gradually give itself over, by 1911, to Gentile's Actualism.[42] This was the time during which the most radical Italian Marxists abandoned much of the materialism of traditional socialism. What they did not abandon was the conception of human beings as species, or communal, beings.

What some of the revolutionary syndicalists proceeded to do was to identify the "communality" of man not with *class*, but with the *nation*. The first intimations of a "revolutionary nationalism" made their appearance among the most radical Marxists. More than that, among syndicalist intellectuals, notions of elitism, political aristocracies, political myths, voluntarism, anti-parliamentarianism, anti-democracy, and mass mobilization became increasingly current. More and more radicals recognized that Italian industry was only marginally developed—and that, as a consequence, a mature, class conscious proletariat was absent. Correspondingly, the entrepreneurial bourgeoisie had not discharged its "historic responsibilities."[43] The economy of the peninsula was painfully retrograde.[44]

Between 1910 and 1914, Italian intellectual life experienced transformative strain. Major Marxist intellectuals, like Roberto Michels, Sergio Panunzio, and A. O. Olivetti, gradually dismantled the old orthodoxies until the crisis of the First World War reduced peninsular socialism to two mutually exclusive revolutionary movements—one, antinational, anticapitalist, and antistate, and the other, nationalist, class-collaborationist, and increasingly statist. Revolutionary syndicalists were to become National Syndicalists—with doctrines that approximated those of the developmental and statist nationalism of Enrico Corradini and Alfredo Rocco.[45] In all of this, human beings were still conceived of as essentially social animals.

During the period immediately prior to Italy's entry into the First World War, the elements of Fascism gradually matured out of the disintegration of positivism and orthodox Marxism. What is remarkable about the period between the founding of *La Voce* in 1909, and the entry of Italy into the war in 1915, was Gentile's anticipation of the revolution that would attend its successful conclusion.

The fact is that by the time Fascism succeeded to power in Italy, Gentile had articulated what was to become, years later, its formal ideology.[46] Years before the other currents that were to inform Fascism matured in the first years of the 1920s, Gentile had already given public expression to what was to become the doctrine of Fascism.

Commencing about the time of the outbreak of the First World War in 1914, Gentile increasingly occupied himself with political commentary and exposition.[47] Actualism was used to come to understand contemporary developments, anticipate events, and propose solutions. Together with the treatment of Italy's immediate concerns, Gentile provided an outline of his conception of the state and the role of the individual in that state. He addressed himself to the making of history—and the role played in history by "great men," who represented in their behavior the prevalent trends of their time.[48]

Gentile anticipated that the war of 1915–1918 would constitute the final phase of the Risorgimento, the restoration of Italy's lost lands and the securing of Italy's political integrity. As such, it would mark the beginning of a new phase in the life of the nation. The Italy that would emerge from the war would no longer be the Italy that had been the "easy prey of foreigners," disdained for its poverty and inertia, a cipher in world affairs.[49]

The Italy that emerged from the war required order, discipline, sacrifice, faith, unstinted labor, and total commitment on the part of all its citizens. That, in turn, required an identification of the individual with the state, a state no longer distant and detached, but one with which the individual could identify, in whose laws the individual could recognize his own will. The "political organization of social life would consist in transcending the dualism of the individual and collective will [in] . . . the state." The individual would obey the state, because the state was the will of his larger self.[50] The state should not be understood as external to the individual—with the individual seen as an abstract particularity. The individual was to be understood as immanent in the ethical community that is the state.[51] Gentile saw the state as that ethical substance to be found at the core of humankind, the living source of each man's personality.[52] During this period, he gave expression, with increasing emphasis, to his conviction that human beings were essentially communal, or social, beings.

If the New Italy was not to serve as the instrument of other, more powerful, economic and political powers, it must renounce all the disabilities of the "old" Italy. If the victorious Italy of Vittorio Veneto was to achieve the stature of a world power, it would have to achieve a new order of discipline and social collaboration.[53] It would have to abandon the old liberal notion that understood individuals as nothing other than rootless particular creatures, indifferent and opposed to a life lived in community.

The New Italy would have to reawaken the conviction that individuals were social beings, that they fulfilled themselves only in community—that outside community they were only "partial beings." In order to do that, the notion that human beings were "species beings" would have to be introduced through the provision of new ideas and a new spirit. Only when Italians identified with their national community, and its executive expression in the state, might the New Italy undertake a postwar expansion of the vast productive capabilities earlier generated to meet the needs of war.[54] Only then might one expect the social reorganization that would integrate all components of the nation into one infrangible unity.

To accomplish all that, Gentile maintained that the "ethical state" was essential. It was that state, animated by "a religious conception of life,"[55] that would communicate the inflexible faith necessary to carry its citizens through the arduous process of regeneration.

In such circumstances, a politically gifted individual would be able to sense the mood of the times and the sentiment of the people—and marshal a nation to the fulfillment of aspirations long held.[56] To be successful, a leader would calculate, assessing trends and measuring tendencies. As is the case in all such circumstances, a real or prospective leader would make all data, all history, his own. Everything would have to be absorbed in living thought. Everything would have to be contemporaneous.

the leader would represent the best of available insights facts into acts

Like all the members of such an emergent ethical community, the leader would represent the best of available insights, assimilating what was external, *facts*, so that they would fuel *acts*. Gentile held that in just such fashion were decisions made. In the process, the enterprise required the review of facts available and an assessment of criteria employed to assign truth status to propositions. Change inevitably and regularly takes place among both categories—and to negotiate the complexities of the modern world, constant vigilance and recalculation is required. At given junctures, choices must be made and responsibilities assumed—and populations must commit themselves.[57]

The more comprehensible these procedures are, the more readily will persons recognize the compatibility of their interests with the interests of the general community, and the more apparent becomes each individual's investment in the state. In the world of common sense, the state is recognized as the ultimate arbiter of force and the executive agent of the nation. The individual identifies with his community. He recognizes it as a community with which he is bound, as though his life is no longer his own, but a spirituality that belongs not only to himself, but to himself in others.[58]

community as state protects the individual & defines through law the options available to him

Beyond that, the community as the state, protects the individual and defines, through law, the options available to him. The state schools the individual to his responsibilities and provides the parameters for acceptable conduct.[59] Gentile argued that the modern state is required to educate citizens to their responsibilities—to awaken the individual to his communal essence. Out of that awakening, a unity would emerge out of a multiplicity—and the sense of community would dilute egoism. What was first seen as opposing externalities would become recognized as an expression of community—and the many would find in unity with the state their most profound selves.[60]

In order to accomplish such a reeducation, the state could not remain "agnostic."[61] The conditions that govern its life require it to assume a moral position concerning virtually every issue. As a consequence, Gentile conceived the modern state to be a "pedagogical state"—morally responsible for the making of "New Men" for a "New Italy." In fact, it can be argued that for Gentile the "New Schools" he proposed long before there was a Fascism would provide the education for the "New State" he anticipated.[62]

By the first years of the 1920s, with the first intimation of Fascism, more and more elements of Gentile's political thought surfaced in the political prose of Mussolini. In the fall of 1921, Mussolini increasingly addressed himself to the "values of the spirit." He affirmed that "Fascists" had "drunken deep of spiritualistic doctrines" from at least the time when "the pseudophilosophy of positivism" reigned unchallenged.[63]

In the beginning of 1922 Mussolini prepared an assessment of "Where is the World Heading?" for the Fascist journal, *Gerarchia*. At that time he opined that all of the political developments of the past century were flanked by a correlative "philosophical process. If it is true," he went on, "that for a hundred years *matter* remained on the altars; today *spirit* is taking its place."[64]

In order that there could be no mistake concerning his intention in using the term "spirit" and "spiritual values," Mussolini had affirmed, a few weeks before, in one of the most important speeches he made before the House of Deputies, that

> It is not only the case that we reject the putative dualism between matter and spirit, we annul the antithesis in the synthesis of the spirit. Only the spirit exists, nothing else; not you, not this room, not the things and the objects that pass before us in the fantastic cinematography of the universe. All that exists, exists only in so far as it is thought, and only when thought, not independently of my thought.[65]

Shortly thereafter, he identified Fascism as a "movement that is intimately, one could say religiously, *idealistic*."[66]

There is very little confusion concerning Mussolini's transit from positivism, through pragmatism, to Bergsonianism, each removing him further from the epistemology and ontology of the materialism so prevalent in his youth. There is no more confusion in the recognition that Benedetto Croce and Gentile influenced him in his development, both directly or through intermediaries like Giuseppe Prezzolini. One need only read the letter from Mario Missiroli—written in August of 1914, when Mussolini was still struggling with respect to his position regarding Italy's entry into the First World War—to document an instance of the influence of Gentile's thought. Missiroli spoke to Mussolini of "creating reality," of "destroying every transcendence," and acknowledging an "absolute subjectivism" as the grounds of knowing and doing. Missiroli went on, in explicitly Gentilean fashion, to speak of the errors of democracy in thinking that the demands of liberty required relaxing the hold of the state over the individual. The theoreticians of democracy, he continued, failed to understand that there was an essential "unity of the citizen with the state"—the "state and the citizen were one single thing." The truth, he continued, was that true freedom obtained only when "every citizen conceived himself the state."[67]

Mussolini was clearly impressed with the letter, and published it in his journal, *Utopia*. All of which makes it reasonably clear that he was under the influence of Gentilean thought throughout the years from about 1908 until the Fascist March on Rome fourteen years later. Throughout those years, Mussolini adopted a number of Gentilean concepts. After the termination of the First World War, for example, he began to regularly speak of Fascism as a "religious" movement,[68] committed to an "intransigent faith" in the nation's future.[69] He spoke of the proposed Fascist state as an "ethical state."[70]

In fact, when Mussolini acceded to power in 1922, and proceeded to put together his first cabinet of ministers, he chose Gentile as his minister of public instruction. When objections were raised, Mussolini insisted that, whatever the circumstances, he would not compromise on that selection; Gentile had been his "teacher."[71]

As soon as Gentile assumed responsibilities in the cabinet of Mussolini, he undertook an increasing number of further obligations. As has already been indicated, Gentile served as president of two commissions devoted to the revision of the Italian Constitution. When he was offered an honorary membership in the Partito fascista nazionale Gentile refused, insisting that he had done nothing to merit it. Instead, he submitted his application to join as a simple member of the Party in the summer of 1923, maintaining that Fascism most closely approximated his views of the world and his aspirations for Italy.

When, in the summer of 1924, the Fascist regime was shaken by the murder of the Socialist deputy Giacomo Matteotti, and many non-Fascist allies began to abandon the regime, Gentile remained loyal. In 1925, he published his *Che cosa è il fascismo*, and organized the meeting that produced, in April 1925, the *Manifesto degl'intellettuali italiani fascisti* (*The Manifesto of Italian Fascist Intellectuals*). The *Manifesto*, that was written entirely by Gentile, was read, slightly revised, and approved by Mussolini—and subsequently published.

The *Manifesto* spoke of Fascism's ideals of personal sacrifice and abnegation in the service of a national ideal—a national ideal that would allow the individual, through his service and sacrifice, to become that which he should be. The *Manifesto* spoke of the religious character of Fascism and its rejection of "liberal agnosticism," predicated as it was on the notion that the state is something extraneous to the individual.

The *Manifesto* spoke of the conflict that preceded Fascism's ascension to power in terms of the activities of the *squadristi*, the action squads of Fascism, as soldiers in the service of a *virtual, revolutionary state*, opposing itself to the anarchism and anti-statism of revolutionary Marxism. In that document, Gentile argued that Fascism was the final resolution of the Risorgimento—the completion of the Italian state. He spoke of Fascism as a faith, a salvific and restorative movement, that found expression in an austere and profoundly spiritual commitment on the part of those young men who had survived the carnage of the trenches during the Great War.[72] In that same year, Gentile founded the Istituto nazionale fascista di cultura which subsequently published a series of major works dealing directly or indirectly with Fascism, its history, its rationale and its accomplishments.

It was during the early years of the 1920s, before and during the Matteotti crisis that threatened the very survival of the regime, that Gentile's ideas had the most influence on Fascism. Until 1925, confined by circumstances, and allied with relatively conservative elements, Mussolini had put together a coalition of factions to rule Italy that settled on an arrangement that looked very much like a traditional authoritarian government for the peninsula. In the summer of 1921, for example, in his first speech to the Chamber of Deputies, Mussolini proposed reducing the Italian state to the dimensions insisted upon by traditional liberals. He spoke of the return of the "Manchestrian state."[73] The talk was of reducing the state to its essential functions—the protection of citizens and their property together with the security of the nation. In December of 1921, the Party Program thus spoke of reducing the state to its "essential juridical and political functions."[74] These postures continued into the first years of the Fascist period.

In June 1924, when the Socialist delegate to the Chamber of Deputies was murdered by Fascist thugs, there had been instant public outrage. While there has never been any credible evidence that Mussolini was directly involved, the regime went into immediate crisis. Many of Fascism's allies abandoned, or distanced themselves from, Mussolini—and there was an increasing sense that the Fascist government was isolated and might fall.[75] Throughout the entire period, Gentile remained resolutely loyal.[76]

The political uncertainty persisted until the turn of the new year. On the 3rd of January 1925, Mussolini assumed full responsibility for the violence that had afflicted Italy throughout the revolutionary interval from 1920 through 1924, but insisted that violence had been necessary to restore Italy to order and fulfill the nation's dream of grandeur and security.[77] Thereafter the regime undertook its consolidation.

What is of significance to the present narrative is the fact that the consolidation which followed involved the abandonment of any notion that the Fascist state, in any sense, would seek to be "Manchestrian" in character. On the 22nd of June, 1925, Mussolini spoke of Fascism as "assuming all power." He spoke of Fascism's "ferocious *totalitarian will*," that sought to make Fascists of *all* Italians—to "fascistize" the nation—so that on some early tomorrow, all Italians would be Fascists.[78]

There was not to be any further allusion to a Fascist "Manchestrian" state. There was only talk of a state commanding unitary discipline, mobilizing all in the service of the state—a state that would defend the nation against the pretenses and duplicities of "hegemonic foreign powers."

After 1925, Fascism took on all the properties that were to define it in history. There was explicit abandonment of any notion of creating a limited, "Manchestrian" state on the peninsula. Fascists were to celebrate the creation of a unique sense of what the *state* was to be. The state, for Mussolini, was no longer to be the "nocturnal watchman" of the political and economic liberals. It was to be a *moral and spiritual reality*, an expression of the historical, linguistic, cultural, political, juridical, and economic history of Italy. For Fascists, the state, animated by a profound sense of unity, was understood to be the "educator of civic virtue, rendering citizens conscious of their historic mission." Italy was to be Fascist, and Fascism was to be Italy. The nation was to be one indissoluble union; the interests of each was to be the interest of all.[79] By 1929, what had emerged from the Fascist revolution was an unmistakable variant of the Gentilean neo-Hegelian state. Mussolini had irrevocably and fully committed Fascism to totalitarianism.

In retrospect, it is clear that the Matteotti crisis of 1924 created circumstances in which Mussolini was compelled to resolve the differences that remained among the disparate elements that had found a place in the Fascism that had acceded to power in October 1922.[80] Among some members of the highest echelons of Fascism there remained syndicalists who entertained reservations about an intrusive state. There were classic liberals who continued to court the political state of the nineteenth century. While many could tolerate a transitional dictatorship, few would surrender to any notion of permanent totalitarian provisions. Circumstances had made a decision necessary. Fascism could no longer pretend to be a traditional or transitional authoritarian regime. Either Fascism was to be an evanescence in the history of Italy, or it was to consolidate itself on a more secure footing. In January 1925, Mussolini opted to seize the future. He reinforced the single-party, dictatorial system he had constructed and infused it with properties that were to give the regime its unique character. Those properties were borrowed from the thought of Giovanni Gentile. They were embodied in the Gentilean notion of *totalitarianism*.

By the end of the 1920s, all these issues had been resolved for Mussolini. He had unequivocally committed himself to the Gentilean notion of the totalitarian state in which "everything [was] in the state, nothing outside the state, and nothing against the state."[81] Fascism was instilled with some of the major convictions of the social and political thought of Gentilean Actualism.

That had become so evident by the early 1930s, that Mussolini charged Gentile with the responsibility of writing the philosophic portion of the official *Dottrina del fascismo* (*The Doctrine of Fascism*)[82] which was to serve as the lodestar of Fascist thought. The *"Idee fondamentali"* (*"Fundamental Ideas"*) of the *Dottrina* were a synoptic presentation of Actualism, and was recognized as such by the Catholic Church.

The Vatican immediately expressed its opposition to the delivery of a philosophical statement of Fascist principles that were clearly objectionable to the Church. The Vatican considered Gentile's Actualism a kind of heretical pantheism, violative of Church dogma. That notwithstanding, Mussolini remained firm in his decision to publish Gentile's account as representative of Fascism's philosophical principles—and the *Dottrina*, with Gentile's statement of "Fundamental Ideas," remains today the definitive statement of the philosophy of Fascism. Gentilean totalitarianism became, and remains, one of the principal defining species-traits of Fascism.[83]

In the "Fundamental Ideas," Fascism was spoken of as a state that was the product immanent in a given system of historical and spiritual forces. Its state system was predicated on a conception of man that

[handwritten margin note: State system based on man that believed reality to be spiritual]

conceived reality to be spiritual. Life was austere, and human beings were understood to be moral entities whose lives transcended the brief compass of material existence to find in a higher spiritual community, not circumscribed in time or space, a life of superior liberty and fulfillment.

The "Fundamental Ideas" described Fascism as "anti-individualistic"—acknowledging "only that individual who identifies himself with the state as the universal consciousness and will of humankind expressed in its particular historic existence." All individuals and categories of individuals, distinguished by their peculiar interests and economic activities, were understood to receive their reality only in the state.

Given the sustaining conviction in the ultimate unity of all in the universal will of the state, *One* person might fully and adequately represent the interests of all. Of all those who are related ethnically and through history, the state creates a nation, "aware of its proper moral unity and will—conscious of its effective existence." For Fascism, the nation as state was understood to be the ultimate source of the moral and intellectual substance of the individual personality. In sum, Fascism was understood not only as the giver of laws and the founder of institutions, but as educator and support of spiritual life. The Fascist state "charged itself with refashioning not only the form, but the content, of life as well—the refashioning of man, his character and faith. To achieve those ends, Fascism requires discipline and authority that reaches deep, unopposed into the spirit."[84]

The entirety of the "Fundamental Ideas" was thus Gentilean in character and expression. Actualism had accorded Fascism its rationale.

It had been Gentile who had argued, years before there was a Fascism, that the state was "the organization and the will of a community"—the agency that would provide for the self-realization of all. To be successful, it would be "necessary that the state subject all to one common will."[85] These were the totalitarian convictions that Fascism was to celebrate throughout its tenure.

After the appearance of the *Dottrina del fascismo* and throughout the 1930s, through the period of political consensus in Italy, when Fascism went essentially unopposed,[86] Gentile continued to loyally serve the regime in an elaborate series of undertakings that supported the effort to render the Partito fascista nazionale the party of all Italians without exception or reservation.[87]

All of this transpired in an enormously complex political environment. Fascist Italy had entered into a vortex of events that, within a decade, were to consume it and change the history of Europe and the world. It was within that whirlwind that Gentile was to live out the remaining years of his life.

7

Fascism and Gentile

By the 1930s, Gentile found himself inextricably embroiled in the complex political environment of Fascism at its apogee. Throughout the entire period, he remained deeply involved in the intellectual defense of the system. For Gentile, Fascism was a political system committed to the moral realization of life's purpose and the renovation and redemption of the nation. His was a image of Fascism as an austere, "religious," philosophy, an expression of a totalitarian conception of life as universal spirit.[1]

In Fascist Italy, Gentile's thought was very widely broadcast. He was charged with the responsibility of directing some of the nation's most prestigeous academic institutions. The publication of the *Enciclopedia Italiana*, under his direction, was one of the most important publications of the period. He controlled his own publishing house, Sansoni, in Florence—and had direct or indirect control over others. He edited, or significantly influenced, a number of professional and popular journals—and, as president of the Istituto nazionale fascista di cultura had ultimate control over much of the literature devoted to Fascist doctrine.

His influence precipitated criticism during this period—for a variety of reasons. Fascists and non-Fascists alike proceeded to mount complaints against the identification of Actualism and Fascism. In order to understand what was involved in those complaints, one has to appreciate something of the intellectual environment of Fascist Italy at that time.

Many Anglo-American intellectuals continue to entertain the notion that intellectuals in Fascist Italy lived under circumstances very much like those that obtained in National Socialist Germany or Stalin's Soviet Union. While the fact is that intellectuals in Fascist Italy were denied the freedom of expression Anglo-Americans have learned to expect in their own liberal environments—intellectuals in Italy were harassed and life was often made difficult—the circumstances were far different than those under which intellectuals lived in Hitler's Germany or Stalin's Soviet Union. Even well-known anti-Fascists like Benedetto Croce survived under Fascist rule and continued to express their opposition, maintaining an elaborate domestic and international correspondence, and, on occasion, leaving the country to later return. A respectable number of intellectuals who had expressed their reservations concerning Fascism, both privately and publicly, managed to survive throughout the tenure of the regime without serious difficulties. Gentile, himself, employed anti-Fascist intellectuals on the staff of the *Encyclopedia Italiana* and published the articles of known anti-Fascists in his journals.

Gentile maintained that he, as a Fascist, expected open and vigorous criticism concerning all matters—even that criticism that was "dissident." His reservations turned on the qualification that all criticism be "constructive."[2] Clearly intellectual freedom was chilled by the portentous suggestion that all discussion be constructive. Nonetheless, Gentile's practice indicates that he was prepared to publish materials that were severely critical of his own position. Throughout its tenure, Fascism allowed a diversity of points of view to find expression in journals and newspapers that were distributed in considerable abundance.[3]

Western intellectuals have found all this difficult to believe. They have all heard, of course, of the death of Antonio Gramsci from tuberculosis in a Fascist prison—and, as a consequence, have assumed that the environment under Fascism approximated that of the then contemporary Soviet Union under Stalin. Nothing could be further from the truth.

In the Soviet Union, even under Lenin, any departures from doctrinal orthodoxy, as defined by the leadership of the Communist Party, brought immediate punishment, expulsion from the party, incarceration, and not infrequently execution. Even the foremost theoreticians of Bolshevism lost their lives in ideological disputes. Trotsky, Bukharin, Kamenev, Zinoviev, and Radek all perished under Stalin. Even before Stalin and his terror, Menshevik theoreticians, Marxists though they were, were executed under Lenin. Bolshevism sustained a "unity of doctrine" by suppressing, incarcerating, or executing anyone who attempted any "deviation." One found very little ideological dispute in the Soviet Union under Stalinism because such discussions were fraught with mortal peril.

While Stalin decimated whole classes of intellectuals,[4] including theoreticians of his own party—even killing, whenever possible, foreign Marxist-Leninists who were "suspect"[5]—there was, very little, if anything, like that in Fascist Italy. Ideological disputes in Fascist Italy had a very different character and a manifestly different outcome.

All of that is now generally recognized. What that means is that doctrinal disputes in Fascist Italy involved something entirely different from those that arose in Hitler's Germany or in the Soviet Union of Josef Stalin. During the period in which Gentile became more and more intensively involved in the intellectual work of the regime,[6] the Roman Catholic Church gradually increased the number and intensity of its objections. As early as 1925, Roman Catholic authors were writing critiques of Actualism that condemned its failure to philosophically provide for a "transcendent God," the God of the Church.[7] In 1929, the Church explicitly expressed its opposition to any attempt by the regime to impose "a totalitarian educational system on the nation"—the clear intention of the Gentilean educational reforms of 1923—the "most Fascist of Fascist reforms." The encyclical *Divini illius Magistri* addressed the entire issue of educational practice. With the passage of time, and as Gentile's influence on the rationale of the regime became more evident, the objections of the Church increased. As Fascism's intentions became more and more clearly totalitarian, the Church recognized that its doctrinal and corporate interests were threatened. With the publication of the official *Dottrina del fascismo* in 1932, there could no longer be any doubt. Fascism meant to dominate Italy and Italians—and Gentile was its spokesman. On the 20th of June, 1934, all of Gentile's works were placed on the Vatican's *Index librorum prohibitorum*. Catholics were proscribed from reading his writings.

Those developments created special problems for Roman Catholics who were Fascists—and political problems for the regime that had concluded its Concordat with the Vatican in 1929. By the mid-1930s, Mussolini made it eminently clear that, for political reasons, he no longer wished to continue to directly and specifically confront the

Roman Catholic Church over the integrity of Fascist doctrine. As a consequence the doctrinal dispute took on a character entirely different from those in other "totalitarian" environments.

For his part, Gentile continued his opposition to the accommodation of Fascism with the Church. Actualism, with its absolute supremacy of the state, allowed little room for accommodation between the state and the Catholic Church. It was nonetheless evident that Mussolini was content to deal with the Church in a less than public display of doctrinal disagreement. That opened space for *Fascist* criticism of Actualism—an eventuality to be expected in the circumstances that typified intellectual life in Fascism Italy.

Throughout the preceding years, *anti-Fascists* like Croce had carried on a running critique of both Fascism and Gentilean thought—but with the changed circumstances of the mid-1930s, *Fascists* who had reason to dissent from Actualism felt themselves empowered to embark on critiques calculated to distance Fascism from Gentile. Among the most vocal critics—not unexpectedly—were Roman Catholics. Even Actualists who had long collaborated with Gentile in his support of Fascism, sought to distance Fascism from his philosophy, in order to avoid a direct confrontation of Fascism with the Mother Church.[8] In those evolving circumstances, Fascists who sought to reduce the friction between the Church and Fascism, or who represented interests that felt threatened by Fascism, could formulate their concerns without conveying the impression that they were opposing the regime. They could insist on their Fascism while at the same time attacking Actualism, reducing what they saw as political or economic threats to some one or another special interest they favored. Armando Carlini was numbered among them.

Carlini had been an orthodox Roman Catholic as well as a convinced Actualist. By the mid-1930s, the social, economic, and political circumstances had so changed within the regime that he felt called upon to attempt a separation of Fascism from Actualism. In his *Filosofia e religione nel pensiero di Mussolini* (*Philosophy and Religion in the Thought of Mussolini*),[9] Carlini proceeded to make the case that Mussolini held fairly traditional views concerning God and the Roman Catholic Church. He fully acknowledged that Mussolini had followed a course that was common among the most important Fascist ideologues, having abandoned positivism, early in the century, in order to assume an increasingly *spiritual* world-view. Carlini also recognized that whatever epistemological notions Mussolini had expressed over the years were clearly *idealist*[10] in character—but he went on to suggest that all that was not sufficient to classify Mussolini as an unqualified philosophical idealist. Idealism was far too "humanistic" in orientation, according to Carlini, to be part of Mussolini's belief system. Philosophical humanism, understood to put emphasis on the human condition rather than a transcendent divinity, would threaten the integrity of orthodox Catholicism.

Carlini argued that the evidence suggested that Mussolini remained "openly Roman Catholic"—certainly, he was not to be identified with the "humanism" and the speculative "pantheism" of idealism—charges that the Vatican, by that time, had leveled against Gentile.

The purpose of Carlini's work was clear. He sought to establish that whatever might be said of Actualism, could not be said of Fascism. As a consequence, if the Church banned Actualism as a heresy, Fascism remained unaffected.[11] That much seems evident. What is perhaps more important, in retrospect, is whether Carlini could really make an effective case and so easily disentangle the two systems.

Carlini went on to argue that the "masterpiece of Mussolinian thought was the Fascist State"—a political conception informed by the philosophical and religious convictions of its founder. Having insisted upon that, Carlini went on to admit that he found himself at a loss when he attempted to fully explicate the "theory" that sustained the reality of the Fascist state.[12] He admittedly had difficulty providing the philosophical rationale for Mussolini's "masterpiece."

Carlini alluded to Mussolini's discourse of the 10th of March, 1929 on the essence of the Fascist state. In that delivery, Mussolini affirmed that Fascism had restored to Italians the proper sense of "the State." The sense to which he referred included the recognition that the state was a "spiritual and moral fact ... a manifestation of the spirit." "It was," Mussolini continued on that occasion, "the bearer of the spirit of a people as it found expression in speech, customs and faith."

For Mussolini, "the State was not only the present, but also the past, and above all, the future. Transcending the brief life of the individual, the State represents the immanent consciousness of the nation. . . . It is the State that educates citizens to civic virtue, instills in them the sense of mission."[13] More than all that, Mussolini had maintained, in the *Dottrina del fascismo*, that the Fascist state was "ethical" in essence and, as such, possessed a moral "personality."[14]

Carlini found himself entirely at a loss to accommodate the character of this "masterpiece of Mussolinian thought" with Roman Catholic notions about the sharp distinction between the responsibilities of the Church and state in Italy. In his discussion, it was transparent to Carlini himself that if the Fascist state was understood to be *totalitarian*, marshalling to itself "all the forces, physical, moral and intellectual of the nation in order to win that conflict that will determine not only the place of the state in the world, but the very course of history itself," it was very difficult to bridge the abyss between Mussolini's views on the state and those of the Church.[15]

Fascism insisted, as Carlini readily acknowledged, that the Fascist state arrogated to itself the responsibility of educating Italians to their moral, social, economic, and political responsibilities. Carlini recognized that for Fascists "everything was to be in the State, nothing outside the State, and nothing against the State." How such an arrangement might be accommodated by a Church that conceived itself *universal*—responsible for the moral and spiritual education of *its* followers was manifestly unclear. The Church insisted on its own independent interpretation of what the "moral life" of its adherents was to be—and how its own institutions were to be governed. Carlini admitted he had no answer to all that. He was "disoriented."[16]

The fact is that there appears to be no way out of the difficulties into which critics like Carlini found themselves. Gentile's critics seemed prepared to contend that one could be, with consistency, both a Roman Catholic and a Fascist. For Gentile, that was not possible. He maintained that "the Church represents . . . a religious position that is in direct antithesis to the conception of the ethical State, founded on a conception of man and of thought, of which religion is the negation." He went on to argue that the "modern state" is informed by a conception that excludes the traditional Church. Whoever speaks of "conciliating" the state and the Church "either does not love the State or does not love the Church." One contemplates "the suppression of the one or the other."[17]

Gentile had no difficulty in considering himself both a Fascist and a Roman Catholic,[18] because Fascism and Roman Catholicism were both *immanent* in his Actualism. His opponents did not have that option. Fascists, who were Catholics, sought the intransigent defense of Fascist doctrine by conceding, as Gentile could not, that individuals possessed "personal integrity" and a "divine essence" independent of the state—an integrity and an essence that required the recognition of a transcendent "Creator."[19] However fervently held, all such notions were in transparent conflict with the official *Dottrina del fascismo*.

These kinds of criticisms were generated by an effort to resolve the tensions between Fascism and the Church and to permit Roman Catholics to be Fascists without the threat of excommunication. Throughout this entire period, spokesmen for the Church continued to identify Gentile's thought as heretical, and it is clear that his views on the absolute sovereignty of the state left scant space for any religion that conceived itself having any absolute value either superior to, or independent of, the state. Should the state, for whatever reason, choose to allow the independent existence of an historic institution like that of the Catholic Church in Italy, it would be at the expense of its sovereignty.[20]

In retrospect, several things are reasonably evident. There were doctrinal disputes among intellectuals in Fascist Italy—and those disputes were permitted. With some important reservations, Fascism's totalitarianism allowed such exchanges. Gentile anticipated them, and he did little, if anything, to attempt their suppression.[21] Gentile expected the process of fusing the individual and the state to be protracted—involving the reeducation of citizens that had long been exposed to liberal "corruption." In the interim, he expected dialogue and doctrinal dispute. All of which suggests something of the singular character of his totalitarianism.

In Fascist Italy, throughout the 1930s, as long as no objections were leveled directly against Mussolini, the Party, or the state, doctrinal disputes were tolerated and sometimes, for one reason or another, solicited. By the mid-1930s, it was reasonably evident that Mussolini and the Party would rather have Gentile suffer the abuse from the institutional Church, and its allies, than have to deal with the Vatican themselves in a major domestic political confrontation.

Thus, in 1940, Carlo Costamagna, a Roman Catholic and a nationalist,[22] as well as a major Fascist theoretician, felt free to direct a number of objections against Actualism. He opened his major work on the doctrine of Fascism by rejecting any notion that "monistic," and "vague" "neo-Hegelianism" might serve as the philosophical foundation of Fascism.[23] At one point, he seemed to reject the Gentilean conviction that the "ethical state" received its moral properties only because the state provided the individual the occasion for his full realization in humanity. Costamagna appeared to reject the notion that the state was an instrumental means to the intrinsically moral purpose of individual self-fulfillment.[24]

In another place, Costamagna appeared to argue that Fascism, as the "new doctrine of the State" conceived the "State as an end in itself."[25] Thus, while he was prepared to admit that the state provided the material conditions for individual existence, and that the state and the individual were interdependent—Costamagna insisted that the individual and the state were *different in nature*. The state, Costamagna held, has ends of its own and could not be identified with the Gentilean "higher self" of individuals.[26] And yet, elsewhere, he argued that "the State is the necessary condition, if not sufficient, for both the existence of the *moral personality* of the individual and the possibility that that personality can evolve to that heroic level . . . *beyond the life of the individual*. That is the ethical foundation of the State."[27] Thus, the reality of the Fascist State was not to be found in the arrangements it had put together to foster and sustain material production, nor in its juridical form, "but in the conception of the world through which it affirms itself."[28] All of which is more than a little obscure.

Fascism, according to Costamagna, was the condition through which individuals reached that level of moral fulfillment that carried them beyond the limits of individual life. The reality of the Fascist state was to be found in its conception of the world. That conception was clearly *religious* in some sense, with the state having, as a consequence, *intrinsically ethical character.* In those circumstances, one would seem to have a choice between established religion or some notion of a *spiritual* state. Nowhere does Costamagna seem to attempt a resolution of that particular dilemma—a dilemma that stalked Fascism throughout its history.

When the English Catholic John Strachey Barnes, in his defense of Italian Fascism, addressed that entire issue, he simply asserted that Fascism had no intention of "divinizing" the state. According to Barnes' account, Fascism fully recognized the existence of a superior and independent moral law to which the state itself must conform. Given that conviction, he held that Fascism and Roman Catholicism were thus fully compatible—and to that end it would be best if Fascism entirely rooted out all of Gentile's thought from the rationale for the regime.[29] That, of course, would seem to identify Roman Catholicism as the conscience of Fascism—a resolution hardly anyone sought.

Together with a number of other Catholic Fascists, what Carlini, Costamagna, and Barnes attempted was to keep the substance of Fascist doctrine while surrendering Actualism. The effort was anything but persuasive. It was difficult to speak of an "ethical or ecclesiastical State," possessed of a "personality," infused with "religiosity," and sustained by "a totalitarian faith"—in which the empirical individual would find "true liberty" and "fulfillment"—without accepting some variant of neo-Hegelianism. Thus, Sergio Panunzio, one of the most able of the Fascist theoreticians—who himself had *political* disagreements with Actualism—insisted that the doctrinal essence of Fascism was to be found in the "philosophical premises of idealism . . . of Vico, Hegel, Mazzini and Gioberti"[30]—the same sources to which Gentile made recourse.

While Panunzio chose not to be drawn into the discussions specifically concerning Gentile, he did affirm that "the Fascist State" shared an indubitable historic connection with Hegelianism—with Fascism, in his judgement, belonging to that form of idealism identified as "transcendent."[31] The problem he alluded to was basically an orthodox religious one. Did the *immanence*, to which Gentile insisted in his philosophical disquisitions, mean to exclude a *transcendent God*? If the answer were yes, it was clear that Actualism was in stark conflict with the established Catholic Church. That created a major political problem for some, perhaps many, Fascists. If Actualism surrendered its insistence on spiritual and religious life being *immanent* in human existence, some way might be found to accommodate the Church without hopelessly impairing the ideology of Fascism.

While all that seems evident, Panunzio's account of a general theory of Fascism is, in terms of its fundamental philosophical principles, inescapably Actualist. For Panunzio, the Fascist State was irreducibly sovereign, intransigently totalitarian, irremediably anti-individualistic, irrepressibly ecclesiastical, insistently pedagogical, and profoundly ethical. Given that constellation of properties, it is hard to imagine what a persuasive rationale for the Fascist state might be if not Actualism.[32] Any such rationale could only resemble that provided by Gentile.

Beyond all these concerns, there were a host of others that fueled the resistance of critics who objected to the role accorded Actualism in the rationale of Fascism. There were *conservative* Fascists who were convinced that Actualists were leading Fascism into some form of "Bolshevik" radicalism—threatening both private property and private economic initiative.

In 1933, Guido Cavalucci delivered an embittered attack on Actualism as a deviant form of Fascism that sought to lead the regime into a system of economic "Bolshevism" that saw the individual swallowed up in the state. Cavalucci argued that there were those who advocated a conception of society and the state that was "entirely collectivist." Within that conception the individual is identified, without remainder, with the state.[33] Cavalucci identified those collectivists as "statists" and "anti-individualists" who sought to abolish private property, and individual rights, in their fevered ideological enthusiasm to fulfill their vision of man as a "communal being." Those collectivists were Actualists who had "contaminated" Fascism with their frenzy.

Cavalucci advocated a return to the convictions Fascism had expressed in the late 1920s and early 1930s, when with the promulgation of the Carta del lavoro (The Labor Charter) Mussolini "respected private property and private initiative."[34] Unfortunately for Cavalucci's argument, by the early 1930s, Mussolini had decided that the "complete organic and totalitarian regulation of production" that had been forthcoming by that time, was not simply a reform, but was a response to the mortal crisis of the capitalist system. Thus, in his speech on the "Corporate State" in November 1933, Mussolini insisted that the "capitalist method of production [had] been superseded, and with it the theory of economic liberalism which was its interpretation and apology."[35]

However much Cavalucci might object, by the first years of the 1930s, Fascism sought to transcend private property, private enterprise and industrial capitalism with an alternative, corporative, system. It was that system—not Actualism—to which Cavalucci really objected. It was a system in which the interests of the individual were "subordinated" to the state. It was a system in which private property, and "private initiative" would lose their institutional protection. By that time, property was seen to have intrinsic obligations to the state, the arbiter of national interest. Fascism had made the transition from the "individualistic conception to the Fascist conception of private property." There were extensive reforms in civil codes and the specific legal rights of property.[36]

That was what critics like Cavalucci sought to resist. Actualism was a convenient pretext. Well into the mid-1930s, they sought to defend the rights of private property and those of individual entrepreneurial initiative. They used objections to the "collectivism" of Actualism to make their defense of quasi-liberalism in the effort to protect their economic interests. It was, in that sense, that such critics argued that Gentilean Actualism approximated Marxist-Leninist Bolshevism.

Cavalucci attributed all the threats mounted against property to be the consequence of the influence of the thought of Gentile and his followers. He argued that Actualism understood the individual to be, in essence, *social*, a communal being, and, as a consequence, Actualism was unalterably socialist in disposition.[37] In fact, Cavalucci specifically argued that Ugo Spirito, a major exponent of Actualism, had attempted to make a case for socialism in the Second Conference of Syndical and Corporative Studies at Ferrara in May, 1932.

The argument was that Actualism sought to undermine the Fascist commitment to "traditional" individualism and private initiative. Cavalucci argued that Actualism failed to appreciate the fact that Fascism was designed to "control" the evils of economic liberalism, not abolish its essentials. Fascism, he insisted, if the influence of Actualism could be neutralized, was designed to *salvage* "capitalist private economy," not suppress it. The course recommended by the Actualists, Cavalucci maintained, with their "integral corporativism," their identification of the individual with the totalitarian state, and their subsumption of all interests to those of the nation, was a prescription for creating an Italian "Bolshevism."[38] Cavalucci maintained that the entire logic of Hegelianism, in its Gentilean form, was anti-individualistic and collectivistic in character. Gentilean social thought, in Cavalucci's judgment, was simply a peculiar variant of socialism.

Perhaps the most curious feature of Cavalucci's criticism of Actualism, as the philosophy of Fascism, was represented in his effort to make the claim that Gentile's thought had actually nothing to do with Fascism. In trying to mobilize an argument against the identification of Actualism with Fascism, Cavalucci quoted extensively from the official *Dottrina del fascismo* that had been *written by Gentile!*[39] Either unprepared to acknowledge, or unaware of the fact, that the *Dottrina* was the work of Gentile, Cavalucci sought to discredit Actualism as Fascism by employing Actualism against itself. The result was most unconvincing.

Both Ugo Spirito and Bruno Spampanato, identified by Cavalucci as Actualist malefactors, made an almost immediate response to his criticism. In their respective replies, both suggested that Cavalucci's opposition to Actualism as the philosophy of Fascism originated in his unreconstructed economic liberalism.[40] Both argued that Fascism had originated in the general antiliberal sentiment found among the radical syndicalists and revolutionary socialists of the first years of the twentieth century. Both argued that Actualism and Fascism found their source in an antiliberalism that was emphatically collectivist in inspiration—and both found that original inspiration in Hegelianism.

For both Spirito and Spampanato, Actualism, like Fascism, was revolutionary. They both maintained that Fascism, from its very founding, sought to transcend traditional political, social, and economic liberalism, and the individualism it had brought in its train. Fascism, they argued, understood liberalism to have been one of the major factors that had weakened the nation and contributed to its inability to resist the impostures of the advanced industrial powers. Spampanato identified Fascism, like Actualism, as a doctrine that sought to escape the "atomistic liberalism" that had disarmed Italy in what was a Darwinian conflict for survival against its more powerful neighbors.

Spampanato, in his final critique of Cavalucci and his objections to Actualism as the philosophy of Fascism, argued that such criticism could only be the product of "preoccupations of the school of economic liberalism," and of those "writers who were ultra-religious."[41] A decade later, that judgment was to be supported by Mussolini himself.

In 1944, Mussolini argued that the defenders of traditional capitalism, and politically committed Roman Catholics, had undermined Fascism throughout its tenure. They had weakened national resolve and had exposed the regime to its mortal enemies.[42] Such opponents had clearly provided some of the support for the anti-Actualism of the mid-to-late 1930s.

Given these considerations, it can be argued that Actualism was, in fact, the philosophical rationale of Fascism. Its critics were those who sought to either reserve a space within its totalitarianism for traditional economic liberalism or for the doctrines of the Roman Catholic Church.

That there were grounds for legitimate philosophical criticism of Actualism, quite independent of the concerns of special interest groups, goes without saying—but it seems reasonably clear that the most explicit, organized opposition, had its source in specific, practical concerns. In terms of Fascism, Actualism seems to have been the only philosophical system that could provide an adequate rationale for the system. That is not to say that there were no *Fascist* objections to

Actualism. There were, in fact, *intransigent* Fascists who mounted opposition to Actualism. During the mid-1930s, Achille Starace, secretary of the Partito nazionale fascista, and Cesare Maria De Vecchi, newly appointed Minister of National Education, both sought to limit the influence of Gentilean idealism among Fascists.[43] The objection was that Gentile had not been sufficiently "intransigent." Non-Fascists and anti-Fascists had been allowed by Gentile to labor in his enterprises. More than that, and as Fascism was drawn further and further into the vortex of international war, Gentile was known to entertain reservations.

Some Fascists refused, apparently for a variety of different reasons, to acknowledge Actualism as the philosophical rationale of Fascism.[44] Like any philosophical system, Actualism could hardly make a convincing argument for its own inerrancy. All that notwithstanding, it remains difficult to imagine a system that might serve persuasively as a rationale for Fascism that did not display the major properties of Gentile's Actualism. Panunzio, in what was one of the last major statements of Fascist doctrine, had made the case that the philosophical rationale of Fascism would have to be some form of neo-Hegelianism. There was no other form of neo-Hegelianism available that might serve Fascism other than that of Gentile's Actualism.[45] Actualism constituted what was perhaps the only coherent philosophical rationale for the totalitarian state.

The claim that the individual had a self-affirming moral imperative to identify with the state—a sovereign state that was the moral embodiment of all the individuals and associations of the nation—a state that had a unique personality, a will and an ethical substance—a state that was intrinsically and exquisitely religious in disposition—all that really had only one plausible philosophical rationale—the reformed Hegelianism of Giovanni Gentile. The reason for that, of course, is not far to seek. The formal rationale for Fascism had been provided by the official publication of the *Dottrina del fascismo* in 1932—written by Gentile himself. Fascism had a philosophical vindication because Gentile had supplied it. That an alternative might be patched together by the critics of Actualism was always very unlikely. Serious Fascist theoreticians, however much they may have resisted Actualism, acknowledged that the unique Fascist doctrine of the state required a neo-Hegelian rationale.

Western academics, inured to the folk-wisdom of contemporary political science—while prepared to accede to the notion that Marxism provided the rationale for Leninism, Stalinism, and Maoism—have systematically denied that Actualism could play any such role for Mussolini's Fascism.[46] While not a single Marxist "charismatic leader" in the twentieth century made revolution in an advanced capitalist country (as Marx prescribed), or undertook the "withering away of the state" (as both Marx and Engels insisted), or insured against the rule of elites (that both Marx and Engels identified as an essential of the "dictatorship of the proletariat"), or provided for the obligatory "rotation in office" (again, as both Marx and Engels insured would be a post-revolutionary feature of socialist society), or resolved the problem of human "alienation" (so emphatically lamented by the young Marx)—Western academics have never hesitated to directly associate Marxism-Leninism, Maoism, Castroism, and even the barbarism of the Khmer Rouge, with the philosophy of Karl Marx and Friedrich Engels.

It takes very little exegesis and comparison to realize that there is more reason to identify Gentile as the philosopher of Fascism than there is to deem Marx and Engels philosophers of Marxism-Leninism. That some, perhaps many, Fascists refused to identify Actualism as the philosophical foundation of their belief system does no more to discredit the association than the fact that many Marxists, including some of the most responsible and profound, refused to recognize Marxism in the belief system and institutional reality of Leninism, Maoism, or Castroism. While there are overt connections between the thought of Mussolini and that of Gentile, it would be very difficult, indeed, to trace the intellectual relationship between Karl Marx and the hermit kingdom of Kim Il Sung or the homicidal barbarism of "Democratic Kampuchea."

There are evident entailments that connect Actualism to the Fascist theory of the state and society. Whatever the difficulties generated by the political, economic, religious and military realities that punctuated Fascism's historic trajectory, the relationship between Fascism and Actualism remained as evident then, as it does today.

8

Gentile and Fascist Racism

After the mid-1930s, Fascist Italy was drawn more and more rapidly into the vortex of what was to become the Second World War. The War in Ethiopia had precipitated the sanctions of the League of Nations and in response, Mussolini gravitated further and further into the orbit of National Socialist Germany. Hitler had supported Mussolini during the crisis precipitated by the Fascist war in the horn of Africa, and Mussolini felt genuine gratitude.

In an international environment dominated by the advanced industrial powers, the war in Ethiopia was part of the geopolitics of Fascism's effort to find its "place in the sun." Not only would Ethiopia provide Italy the resources its industries sorely lacked, but ports on the Eastern shore of the horn of Africa would provide access to the Indian Ocean, by-passing the English controlled Suez Canal.[1] Italy would no longer be a "prisoner" in the Mediterranean, closed in on the West by Britain's control of Gibraltar and on the east by its control of Suez. With ports opening out into the Indian Ocean, Italy could, once again, aspire to mercantile power. The Italian peninsula might serve, as it had in its past, as a world trading center, a seedbed of a "new civilization." Italy, as a Third Rome, would be propelled into the ranks of the "great powers." After 1935, Mussolini put plans into motion designed to provide Italy hegemony in the Mediterranean.[2]

The war in Spain, that soon followed the conquest of Ethiopia, would provide Italy with an ally on the Atlantic Ocean, outside the confines of Gibraltar.[3] Fascism would no longer have to fear economic blockade by the "demoplutocracies," the industrialized "imperialist" powers that had, in Mussolini's judgment, attempted to thwart the rise of renascent Italy.

In October and November 1937, Mussolini spoke of a "necessary alliance" with Germany and Japan in anticipation of what he conceived an inevitable conflict between the "proletarian nations" and the "sated" industrial powers. It would be a "war necessary in order to break through the crust which [was] stifling the energy and the aspirations of . . . young nations."[4]

On the 6th of November, the "Anti-Comintern Pact" between National Socialist Germany, the Empire of Japan, and Fascist Italy was signed—to be followed by the "Pact of Steel" in May 1939—tying Italy's future irrevocably to that of Hitler's Germany. For Giovanni Gentile, that union brought fateful consequences in its train.

In the course of all the developments that took place through 1935 to 1939, two influences emerged that were to impact on doctrinal developments in Fascist Italy: (1) the conquest of Ethiopia had exposed Fascist Italy to the prospect of protracted contact between Italian citizens and an indigenous non-European population; and (2) the increasingly intimate contact between Fascism and National Socialism produced political pressures for an ideological accommodation between the two that would make their political and military union "totalitarian." For the first time in the history of Fascism, in the pursuit of just that totalitarian union, biological racism and anti-Semitism made an appearance among Fascist thinkers.

After the conquest of Ethiopia, Mussolini blamed unrest in the new colony on the failure of Italians to maintain the appropriate detachment from the local population. Consorting with indigenous women, as a case in point, thoroughly undermined the social distance Mussolini felt Italians were required to maintain if they were to be the "civilizers" of backward nations. Mussolini was outraged by the coarse behavior of both Italian military and civilian personnel who violated the norms of conduct deemed appropriate by the people of Ethiopia. The local population had quickly lost their respect for the Italians, together with any possible notion that the victorious Italians were in any sense their "superiors."[5] Mussolini sought an immediate remedy in the promulgation of racist legislation designed to restrict other than officially regulated contacts between the Italians and the local population.

Together with these developments, Fascist relations with Italy's Jewish population were influenced by increasingly intimate contacts between National Socialists and Fascists. Some Fascists quickly imagined that increasing concern with the "Jewish question" would reduce the distance between Rome and Berlin. Anti-Semitism was so central an issue in the ideology of Nazi Germany that the conviction was held by many that Fascist Italy would have to make some gestures concerning the Jewish question in order to gratify the Germans. Roberto Farinacci, one of Fascism's "elder statesmen," proposed anti-Semitic legislation in order to convince the Germans that Italy was serious in its fateful pact with National Socialism. The motive was strictly political—having little, if any, theoretical or "philosophical" rationale. More and more Fascists agitated for an appropriate formulation of a specifically Fascist position on the Jewish question.

Before the late 1930s, Mussolini had never betrayed any evidence of anti-Semitism. Until that time, in fact, Fascist Italy had provided more refuge for Jews fleeing National Socialism than almost any other nation.[6] With respect to the issue of Italian Jews, Mussolini argued, in December 1937, that there were not many Jews in Italy, and "with some exceptions, there is no harm in them." As late as the 13th of February, 1938, he reassured Margherita Sarfatti that his views concerning what should be done with respect to the question of Italian Jews were "moderate." Irrespective of pressures that were mounting throughout the system, he maintained that he had no intention of creating problems where there were none.[7]

The evidence suggests that Mussolini's decision to make some form of racism and anti-Semitism an integral part of Fascist ideology was made in the summer of 1938. The decision was part of a resolution governed almost entirely by Fascist foreign policy concerns.

In March, German troops had marched into Austria and the *Anschluss* with Germany was realized. That impacted on Mussolini's judgments concerning Italy's immediate interests. The German initiative convinced Mussolini that between 1934 and 1938, the international situation had been completely transformed. Germany and Italy had been drawn together by the opposition to both dictatorships by the industrialized democracies. Both had chosen to defy them; Italy by pursuing its goals in Ethiopia, and Germany by its union with Austria.

In May 1938, Hitler visited Rome and Mussolini was informed that Germany intended to take up the cause of the Sudeten Germans in Czechoslovakia—a decision that might lead to an international crisis before the end of the year. The time frame within which the "inevitable war" with the industrialized democracies would take place was foreshortened.

For Mussolini, it became apparent that war in Europe was very probable, if not imminent, and that an alliance with Hitler's Germany was the only option available if Italy was to seek mastery in the Mediterranean.[8] As a consequence, he felt that the removal of any impediment to complete collaboration between the two totalitarian-isms had to be removed.

It had been brought to Mussolini's attention that in the past, meet-ings between German and Italian representatives sometimes involved Nazis having to directly negotiate with Italian representatives who were Jewish. It was felt that such "embarrassments" created unneces-sary distrust on the part of the Germans and made contacts "uneasy." The consequence was that as early as 1936, Mussolini had ordered that the Italian ministries not send Italian Jews to Germany on official missions. It was clear that such an order could only be a stopgap measure—but it did constitute the first official act of anti-Semitism on the part of the Fascist government—and it prefigured what was to come.

By the summer of 1938, it seemed expedient that the Jewish ques-tion no longer be allowed to create problems of any sort between National Socialist Germany and Fascist Italy. The consequence was the publication of the "Manifesto of Fascist Racism" on the 15th of July.[9] Written by a young anthropology student, with Mussolini's guid-ance, the Manifesto was not at all transparent. Its full intent was un-certain.

The Manifesto, itself, and the subsequent Fascist commentaries, illustrate how difficult it was for Fascism, whatever the practical in-centives, to incorporate anthropological racism into the established ideology. Almost immediately, in the official Party press, readers were told that Italian racism, although vaguely predicated on "biological data," was not to be understood as "narrowly materialistic," but as "essentially humanistic," and "fundamentally spiritualistic"—meant to uplift Italians to their fullest moral responsibilities.[10]

Whatever evidence is available, suggests that both Fascists and non-Fascists alike were surprised by the regime's decision to embark on racism of whatever sort. To all those Italians in any way involved with the issue, the immediate threat of anti-Semitism was more than dis-concerting. Italy's forty-five or fifty thousand Jews were well-assimi-lated.[11] The number of Italian Jews who were members of the Fascist Party exceeded their ratio in the population,[12] and it is clear that for years Mussolini considered Italian Jews facilitators of Italian culture to the outside world.

For years after Nazi persecutions began, thousands of Jewish refugees from Northern Europe were welcomed in Italy. That was to change with the promulgation of anti-Semitic legislation in the fall of 1938. Jews were to be denied positions in the schools and universities as well as the armed services.[13]

The clear purpose was to assure that no Italian Jews would interface with their German counterparts in any official cultural, military, or political exchanges. What shocked Italians, both Fascists and non-Fascists, was the recognition that Jews were to be excluded from such contacts not because of something they had done, but for whom they were. All of which seemed to violate some of the most fundamental principles of Fascist ideology concerning personal responsibility and the rejection of materialist determinism.

For Gentile, the notion that a collection of persons could be held, in some sense, guilty simply because they were members of a historic community was unimaginable.[14] Gentile had never displayed the least prejudice against any racial, national, or ethnic group. He had certainly never shown any antipathy toward Jews. Throughout the years in which Gentile served as director of a variety of cultural and professional institutions there was never any evidence of anti-Semitic discrimination. For Gentile, the doctrinal developments precipitated by events were to create critical moral issues. He had never given any evidence of anti-Semitism. In the early 1930s, the article, "Anti-Semitism," prepared for the *Enciclopedia Italiana*, was prepared by the Jewish Italian, Alberto Pincherle; the article "Hebrews," was prepared by the Jewish Italian G. Levi Della Vida; and in the article "Race," the scientific objections to National Socialism racism were fully articulated.[15] In 1937, in Gentile's journal, *Giornale critico della filosofia italiana*, German anti-Semitism was identified as a "monstrous barbarism" inappropriate to a civilized society.[16]

Throughout his career, Gentile worked intimately and extensively with Jewish scholars from a variety of countries. With the rise of German anti-Semitism in the 1930s, he facilitated the placement in Italy of Jewish refugees. Paul Oskar Kristeller was one of those refugee scholars with whom Gentile shared an intimate work relationship. Gentile sought to secure him Italian citizenship, and when that subsequently became impossible, he assisted him with funds to underwrite his emigration to the United States. Italian Jews like Giorgio Fano, Rodolfo Mondolfo, Gino Arias, Giorgio Mortara, Emilio Servadio, and Attilio Momigliano have testified to Gentile's assistance and support.

The promulgation of racist and anti-Semitic legislation in the fall of 1938 thus created very grave moral, intellectual, and political problems for Gentile. It was evident that racism of whatever sort was inimical to Actualism. Every and any form of materialism was anathema to Gentile's absolute idealism[17]—and that repugnance had been built into the official *Dottrina del fascismo*. In 1929, Balbino Giuliano, one of Gentile's students could write, for example, that among the "duties of Fascists" was the recognition that "all human beings deserve our respect if only because they are human and carry, as we do, the mark of divine creation."[18]

It was almost immediately evident that Fascism could not incorporate the biological racism or pathological anti-Semitism of National Socialist Germany into its ideology without grievous moral tension. Many factors probably contributed to that circumstance.

Italy had little history of racism or anti-Semitism. Although there was some Roman Catholic anti-Semitism during the last half of the nineteenth century, in general Italian anti-Semitism had shallow roots. As has been indicated, Italian Jews had been well assimilated and they were to be found throughout the economy, the political system, and the military establishment. To all that, the influence of Gentile's Actualism, throughout the 1920s, and until the later 1930s, must be added.

From the turn of the century forward, Gentilean idealism had a profound impact on intellectually aggressive Italians. By the early 1920s, even foreigners recognized that Italian idealism had become a dominant intellectual influence in Italy.[19] By the early 1930s, Actualism had imparted a specific moral character to Fascism. There was an explicit rejection of any form of materialism and determinism, combined with an emphatic commitment to personal responsibility. The result was that Fascist racism, throughout its historic trajectory, sharply distinguished itself from the racist determinism of Hitler's National Socialism.[20] That distinction influenced not only the content of Fascist racism, but Fascist practice as well. For all its enormity, Fascist racism (certainly until the collapse of the regime in July 1943) did not lend itself to organized violence against Italian Jews.

There were scattered incidents of anti-Semitic violence in Italian cities after the introduction of official anti-Semitism, for example, but Fascist officials almost invariably intervened to protect victims. Physical attacks on Jews were relatively rare and almost invariably had their sources in personal grievances—and almost always were suppressed by official Fascist intercession.

Initially, throughout the first years of the Second World War, the offices of the Fascist Foreign Ministry, together with orders conveyed to the Italian military command, served to protect Italian Jews in those countries occupied by German forces. Subsequently, Albanian and Tunisian Jews were similarly protected, and both territories became sanctuaries for Yugoslavian and Bulgarian Jews escaping German anti-Semitism. Ultimately, the Italian Foreign Ministry protected non-Italian Jews fleeing German forces in France, Yugoslavia, and Greece. At the same time, the Fascist Internal Ministry allowed non-Italian Jewish refugees to enter Italy, rejecting German requests for their extradition. In Italian occupied France, the police forces of Fascist Italy protected Jewish places of worship that had become centers of refuge for Jews escaping both the authorities of Vichy France and the German military. National Socialist officials appealed directly to Mussolini in their effort to stop such "anomalies," but to no avail.[21]

How much of this can be attributed to the fact that for years Gentile maintained a virtual monopoly over the cultural life of Italy,[22] and that the influence of Gentilean humanism had made the entire notion of racism and biological determinism fundamentally antithetical to Fascist doctrine, is impossible to argue with any confidence. Nonetheless, Fascist behavior with respect to the Jews, Italian or non-Italian, saved many thousands from the Nazis. What seems clear is that some of the most important members of the Fascist hierarchy, including Mussolini, himself, resisted the most malevolent implications of the racist legislation for which they had been responsible. However much Fascism became dependent on Hitler's Germany, there forever remained a determined resistance to its racist barbarism.

For Gentile, himself, the introduction of racial and anti-Semitic legislation created moral problems of unimaginable magnitude. His views on racism and anti-Semitism were universally known. After the passage of the racist legislation of 1938, he continued, with discretion, to assist Jewish scholars who had lost their positions. He had always maintained that one's duty to the state required working within the system in order to redress grievances. He complied with the new racist statutes, but sought within those confines to do whatever he could to provide assistance to Jewish scholars. He continued to extend protection, assisting them in the publication of their work, providing employment on the staff of the *Encyclopedia Italiana*, and furnishing recommendations for other Jewish scholars who sought to emigrate.[23] There is some evidence that Gentile remained loyal to the regime because he was convinced that he could thereby more effectively influence subsequent developments.[24] As late as May 1943, at a commemorative conference for Michele Barbi, Gentile made public references to his Jewish teacher, Alessandro D'Ancona, affirming that anyone who had known him and benefited from his instruction could not abandon his memory because of circumstances. That would be, Gentile insisted, "unconscionably vile."[25]

As the regime sank deeper and deeper into the catastrophe that was the Second World War, Gentile continued his work as a Fascist intellectual. As it became more and more apparent that the war was going disastrously for the Axis powers, many elements within the Party and the regime became increasingly restive. There were youth groups who sought to "reenergize" the "revolution" by abandoning the "formalistic morality" of Actualism. Others sought an identification with Hitler's Nazism.

From the war's very commencement, Gentile had misgivings. He was known to have serious reservations concerning Fascism's alliance with Nazi Germany. Unlike his active endorsement of Italy's involvement with the First World War, Gentile made no public statements concerning Italy's participation in the Second. Although deeply grieved by Italian reverses, Gentile occupied himself almost exclusively with his intellectual and cultural activities to the exclusion of those that could be identified as primarily political.[26]

As Italy's military situation worsened and Allied forces drove Italo-German forces from North Africa, and Italy itself became directly threatened, the Fascist Party called on the nation's intellectual leadership to attempt a reanimation of spirit among Italians in the expectation that an armed defense of national territory was imminent. Public morale had fallen to threatening levels. It was at that point that Carlo Scorza, secretary of the Fascist Party, called on Gentile to provide a public expression of his continued faith in the nation's future.

Gentile was one of the few Fascist intellectuals to respond to Scorza's call. On the 24th of June, 1943, he delivered his address, "Il Discorso agli Italiani (A Speech to Italians)"[27] in which he reaffirmed his Fascist commitments, but proceeded to speak to all Italians, Fascist or not. He repeated all those convictions that had been embodied in his political writings. While he spoke of the errors of Fascism—he made no mention of those racial policies he clearly deplored. He spoke of the effort to make of the nation a "greater and immortal Italy"—a goal for which one must be prepared to live, labor, and if necessary, die. It was a call to renewed commitment in the pursuit of a victory against the international oppressors of yesterday.

One of the consequences of his speech was the receipt of death threats from elements that sought an early end to the conflict. Gentile made no mention of the threats; they were found among papers left to his heirs after his death.

Approximately one month later, on the 25th of July 1943, following the Allied landings in Sicily, and the bombing of Rome, the king, in a meeting he called, suggested that Mussolini resign. Mussolini refused, but was arrested and transferred to a prison off the coast of Sardinia. General Pietro Badoglio was appointed prime minister and Raffaele Guariglia, foreign minister. Guariglia immediately began secret negotiations for the unconditional surrender of Italy to the Allies. On the 8th of September, the Badoglio government announced that a treaty of peace had been signed. The German response was to send troops to occupy the peninsula and proceed to rescue Mussolini from his prison. Mussolini was flown to Munich to meet with Hitler. On the evening of the 18th of September, Mussolini broadcast a speech to the Italian people announcing that he had formed a new government in the north of the peninsula that would continue to honor Italy's obligations to its German ally.

Until Italy's surrender and subsequent decision to become a co-belligerent against its former German allies, Gentile had been a staunch monarchist. In the interim between the collapse and the announcement of the formation of a new Fascist republican government in the north, Gentile had simply remained at his post.

With the establishment of the Fascist republican government, the prospect of serving that government became a real possibility for Gentile. All of his closest associates, including Ugo Spirito, counseled against his involvement. In November, Mussolini asked if Gentile would meet with him. On the 17 of November 1943, the two met for two hours in what Gentile called "an emotional encounter." Mussolini requested nothing of Gentile; his aides later suggested that Gentile serve as president of the Accademia d'Italia in order to sustain the cultural continuity of Italy. With his acceptance, Gentile became directly associated with the Fascist Social Republic of Salò.[28] On the 28th of December, he published an article in which he expressed his sense of what the situation demanded.

Gentile recommended a "pacification of hearts" among Italians of whatever political beliefs. He called for a commitment to national unity that would supercede loyalty to any party. He urged that unity in the face of the threat of extinction that hung over the nation. He recognized that there were "so many faults to expiate, so many wrongs to redress; so much evil for which we will be reproved by a dutiful examination of conscience."[29]

In November, Mussolini had spoken of "humanism and Mazzinianism in its spiritual essence" as among the "highest realizations of Fascism."[30] Gentile had some reason to believe that his views would influence developments within the evolving tragedy.

Throughout the territories not yet occupied by the Allied armies that were forcing their way up the Italian peninsula, together with the indecisiveness, confusion, and sporadic violence that attended the process, there had already been a wave of conciliatory sentiment among Italians of all political orientations. In Venice, Florence, and Modena, political prisoners were released and there were meetings between the most diverse factions in the effort to reorganize against the avalanche of misfortune.[31] Even some Communists and socialists had rallied around the Fascism that was in the process of reconstituting itself. Nicola Bombacci, one of the original founders of the Italian Communist Party came to serve Mussolini as an adviser,[32] together with socialists like Carlo Silvestri and Ottavio Dinale.[33]

With the events of July 1943, the original Fascism had dissolved. Almost all the major figures of the regime that had governed Italy for twenty years disappeared into anonymity. With the return of Mussolini in September, very few of the major intellectuals of the immediate past had resurfaced. Other than Gentile, there were very few others. Many far lesser lights reappeared in the massive confusion that characterized the attempt to reconstruct a government for the north of Italy. They were to attempt to impose their own convictions on the emerging system. Some of the most important shared a clutch of features: (1) they were almost all, with few exceptions, "intransigent," that is to say, they all sought vengeance against those who had "betrayed" the fatherland and Fascism; (2) they were almost all pro-German, either because Fascist Italy had committed its honor to the alliance, or because only the victory of Nazi Germany could salvage the nation's future. Individuals such as Alessandro Pavolini and Roberto Farinacci embodied both convictions. Both had attempted to organize a "Provisional Fascist Government" while Mussolini was still incarcerated. During that interval, they had sought safe haven among the Germans. With Mussolini's reappearance, Pavolini was declared "provisional party secretary" and Farinacci sought appointment as minister of the interior. Farinacci made his position eminently clear. He intended to remain "loyal and unequivocal—with [Fascism's] German comrades."[34] Pavolini was no less unequivocal. He sought the immediate and merciless punishment of all "traitors."

Together with elements represented by Pavolini and Farinacci, there was another very exiguous minority, totally committed to Hitler's National Socialism, and wedded to his anthropological and biological racism—with all its "scientific materialism," determinism, and notions of racial inferiority. Giuseppe Preziosi led that group and was its spokesmen. All of which was to have very grave implications for Gentile's concept of Fascism and for Gentile himself.

Almost immediately upon the effort to reconstitute Fascism through a "Fascist Republican Party," Gentile became the object of attack. During December 1943 and January 1944 at the same time that Gentile was calling for a "pacification of hearts"—and both Fascists and socialists in places like the Romagna were appealing to Mazzinian ideas of national interest—Preziosi sent a long memorandum to Mussolini calling for a final solution to the Jewish question. In that memorandum, one of the first persons named as an enemy of such a resolution was Gentile—who was charged with having made the cultural and Party institutions he directed veritable "houses of Hebrews."[35]

Mussolini, for personal and political reasons, sought to marginalize Preziosi and his pathologies. Preziosi, however, had the support of important members of the German political and military command in Italy, as well as members of the Nazi hierarchy in Berlin, including Joseph Goebbels and Hitler himself. Mussolini was compelled to tolerate Preziosi although he resisted his most obscene interventions.[36] Nonetheless, the Program of Verona, that was to serve as a provisional constitution for the Fascist Republic, divested Italian Jews of their citizenship, exposing them to a level of discrimination that was to threaten their very survival.[37]

Throughout the fall and winter of 1943 and 1944, Gentile continued his enjoinments of pacification, his reiteration of the mistakes and moral failures of Fascism that demanded "expiation." He spoke of the community of interests of all those "born in the same land"—whose moral principles and intelligence would unite everyone in their pride of being Italian. Morality and intelligence would avoid the horrors of civil war, uniting all members of the national community, in a "consensus" that would restore, once again, "order and justice."[38]

All of this was generic Gentile. The recourse to morality and intelligence had been a common theme of all of Gentile's philosophical and political writings for almost half a century. Gentile remained uncharacteristically circumspect in addressing the racism and anti-Semitism he clearly deplored. Only his final lecture, "Giambattista Vico," provides evidence of his intentions.

Once again, Gentile did everything he could to avoid directly confronting the Fascism to which he had given his allegiance and for which he felt, in part, morally responsible. In his delivery before the Accademia d'Italia, on the 19th of March 1944, less than one month before his assassination, Gentile traced, once again, the history of philosophy that concluded, in his judgment, in Actualism, and by implication, Fascism. It is of considerable significance that in tracing the course of that long trajectory Gentile included the thought of Baruch Spinoza, the Jewish philosopher.[39] The fact that Gentile had done that, in circumstances in which Jews had been identified as members of an "enemy nationality," was a matter of some consequence.

In 1938, Carlo Costamagna—as we have seen one of the major anti-Actualists who emerged in the late 1930s—had charged Gentile with having infected the youth of Italy with conjectures about international philosophical development that included the "corrosive" influence of the Jew Baruch Spinoza.[40] There was a public exchange at the University of Milan between those who insisted upon, and those against, the identification of the thought of Spinoza with "Jewish perversion." Gentile could only be aware that any mention of Spinoza was a matter of political significance.

Gentile was fully aware of the implications of making positive reference to Jewish philosophers. During the height of the anti-Semitic campaign he had paid tribute to the memory of his Jewish teacher Alessandro D'Ancona in a manner that left no doubt about his positive assessment.[41] It was an affirmation that ensured the increased enmity of opponents like Giovanni Preziosi. To have once again referred to Jewish thinkers without charging them with the "corruption" of non-Jews was something that was not done thoughtlessly.

By 1944, there were very powerful forces within the ranks of renascent Fascism that were violently opposed to Gentile. Gentile was fully apprized of the threats he ran in the tragic circumstances that had swept over Fascism and Italy. It seems that what he sought was to make clear his identification with the Fascist "moderates" against the "intransigents" and "intolerants" who had made vengeance and anti-Semitism irreplaceable components of Republican Fascism. He continued to follow his strategy of attempting to reform Fascism from within rather than the damage its survival capabilities.

So great was the enmity of the intransigents toward Gentile that when Gentile was assassinated on the 15th of April 1944, Mussolini immediately ordered an inquiry in order to determine whether any Fascist elements were involved. The assassins were determined to have been Communists.

When he was assassinated, Gentile had been on his way to intercede for students and university faculty who had been charged with anti-Fascist activities. Even representatives of the non-Fascist and anti-Fascist community deplored the pointless violence. Mussolini was deeply moved by the murder. As a reprisal, the authorities arrested three academics known for their anti-Fascism, but the Gentile family pleaded for their release—maintaining that Gentile had worked for a pacification of hearts and the reconciliation of all Italians. The hostages were duly released.

Mussolini ordered the provincial authorities to inter Gentile's body in the cathedral of Santa Croce in Milan.[42] He was interred beside the remains of some of Italy's most illustrious sons.

9

Conclusions

Long before there was a Fascism, Gentile was its philosopher. That can be said because of several intersecting realities. By 1921, Gentile was one of the most influential thinkers in Italy.[1] Certainly there were few intellectuals who had wider impact. That must be understood in a context that found several lines of political thought converging to produce the elements of an innovative national socialism that was to reveal itself as remarkably attractive to revolutionaries throughout the twentieth century.[2]

Gentile's speculative system satisfied some of the critical intellectual and mobilizational needs of that emerging synthesis. Italy was then a new nation aspiring to take its place among the "great powers." In the peninsula's north, the first efforts at comprehensive industrial development had achieved some notable results. Although desperately poor, Italy sought to overcome those limitations that had made of it a nation of secondary or tertiary importance among those that dominated international life. In a world largely ruled by the imperialist powers, Italy was making the first tentative moves in asserting itself.

Doctrinal nationalism accompanied the process. As early as 1907, Italian nationalists spoke of what was required to create the necessary, if not sufficient, conditions for "a future of prosperity, of power and of grandeur" for the nation.[3] Intellectual activists like Giuseppe Prezzolini and Giovanni Papini called for a "new nationalism" that would generate the will and the energy for the rapid industrialization and economic growth of the peninsula.[4]

Everyone committed to the notion of the rapid growth and industrialization of Italy recognized that the effort would require massive investments of enthusiasm, dedication, and sacrifice—the only capital that might be forthcoming on the impoverished peninsula. All, with few exceptions, anticipated the construction of necessary institutions to foster and sustain the effort. Among those institutions, the state was considered paramount. Long before the First World War, Italian nationalists argued that in order to foster and sustain the process of development, the state would have to be understood as a sovereign institution "conceived as a *person* distinct from its subjects, which serves not only as guardian of its present and future members, but of its own particular interests as well."[5] It was held that only then could the state discharge those demanding functions central to the creation of a modern and powerful nation.

In all of this, it was accepted that individual and special parochial interests would have to be subordinated to the general process of creating a "Greater Italy." "Individuals," it was said, "are . . . organs or instruments for national ends and the nation must concern itself with their wellbeing only in so far as they can be made to be more efficacious and more serviceable in its life."[6] Unmistakably anti-liberal and anti-democratic, these were the central features of a rising revolutionary sentiment.

For Gentile, and for the intellectuals who initially committed themselves to Fascism, Mussolini and his movement embodied Italy's effort to find its place in the sun in a world environment in which all the advanced industrial powers had already established themselves. From his earliest youth, Gentile sought the rehabilitation of Italy—so long, in his judgment, the victim of foreign oppression.[7]

In that sense, Gentile's Actualism was one with the evolving National Syndicalism, Nationalism, and Futurism that all fed into the Fascism that emerged at the conclusion of the First World War.[8] For Gentile, the Italy that was emerging from the Great War was an Italy that required a "sober sense of life"—a recognition that life was sacrifice and commitment. For a nation without natural resources and without capital, having only unskilled labor and will as assets, a philosophy of sacrifice and enterprise was essential. More than that, the order and stability that might be forthcoming from a "strong state" clearly recommended itself. Gentile's Actualism provided all that.

The political genius of Mussolini lay in his ability to recognize the serviceability of Actualism. By the end of the First World War, Mussolini perceived that the philosophy of Gentile supplied the rationale for the system he sought to put into place. However those of us in democratic environments assess what transpired thereafter, it is evident that Gentile's thought supplied the rationale for Fascism.

This was the environment in which Gentile developed his system. For our purposes here, a systematic critique of Gentile's metaphysics or his political philosophy would exceed the limits of space and patience. For the purposes of the present account, it is only necessary that we come to understand something of how Actualism came to occupy the place it did in Fascist doctrine—and when and how we might expect to see its equivalent again.

Gentile saw Actualism as a more coherent, because more intelligible—and more defensible, because more moral—rationale for developmental nationalism. He argued for the "tutelary" state—not because the state was an end in itself, or even because the state was instrumental for national purpose—but because he conceived the state and the individual as *one*—united because the ultimate purpose of the union was the full moral development of each individual within the ethical state. The ultimate interests of both were, in essence, identical. In that sense, Actualism afforded Fascism a consistency it would otherwise not have.

Most ethicists recognize the merits of making moral systems rest on some unproblematic intrinsic value like self-fulfillment. Thus Gentile, in his final apologetic for his Fascism, maintained that "in seeking to define the moral law, it can be expressed as strictly as possible in the admonition: fulfill oneself as a human being [*sii uomo*]."[9] Mussolini had early identified the same imperative at the normative base of political ethics: "Our morality says to man: behave in accordance with your conscience and fulfill yourself as a human being [*sii uomo*]."[10]

In essence, what Gentile had done was to provide the philosophical and ethical rationale for a form of the political state with which the individual could fully identify. Rather than the sociological, ethnic, economic, and political rationale common among nationalists of the period, he generated an entirely neo-Hegelian idealistic interpretation of the character of both the nation and the state. More than that, his conception of the relationship between the individual and the state was shaped by activity, faith, service, sacrifice, and selfless labor—the requisite virtues of persons caught up in a forced-draught process of economic growth, expansion, technological innovation, and moral renewal.

The coming of the Great War—which was to produce the hundreds of thousands of restless combat veterans—found some of the most important elements of the Italian population already infused with an enthusiasm for developmental nationalism. Moved to political activism by high emotional salience, it was not difficult for many nationalists to immediately perceive the virtues of Gentile's Actualism. Long before Gentile formally identified himself with Fascism, many Fascists were familiar with his ideas. For Fascists, Gentile's Actualism provided the moral and philosophical substructure for a system of thought Mussolini had already fabricated out of the convictions of the heretical Marxism of National Syndicalism. It was the final component of the synthesis that informed the totalitarian rule of Italy throughout the interwar period.

In general, scholars who have dealt with the Fascist phenomenon, have acknowledged that without Actualism, Fascism would have no sustaining intellectual rationale.[11] In that sense, Gentile served Fascism as Marx served Marxist-Leninist systems. Giovanni Gentile was, in effect, the "philosopher of Fascism."[12]

That Fascism, in practice, departed from the ideals of Gentile goes without saying.[13] However true, what appears equally evident is that Actualism served not only as Fascism's rationale, but its conscience as well. Gentile did not hesitate to refer to Fascism's "errors" and "evils." His very doctrine made Fascists and non-Fascists alike aware of the obligations of the regime. For Gentile, the acknowledgement of error, and evil, was an affirmation that Fascism never *was*, it was always in the process of making itself.

What made Gentile a Fascist, and caused him to remain a Fascist until his death, was a conviction that the "materialistic plutocracies" that opposed Fascism, and renascent Italy, were the progenitors of a style of life that promised only decadence and moral decay. In his judgment, a victory of plutocratic "democracy" or Marxist "proletarianism" over Fascism would condemn Italy and the world to an extended period of singular debasement.

It was for that reason that, irrespective of the fact that he found biological racism and anti-Semitism abhorrent, Gentile remained loyal to the system. While many Fascist intellectuals had abandoned the regime for a variety of reasons, for Gentile, to have done that, would have belied the moral convictions of a lifetime. During the final agonies of the regime he served, and for which he ultimately sacrificed himself, he could only comfort his children by telling them that he could only do what he had to do. "I must go where my conscience leads me," he told them, "That is what I have preached all of my life."[14]

Choices of these kinds are to be found throughout the history of politics. They are choices made by honest and moral men in morally troubled and conflicted times. For Gentile, Fascism embodied his hopes for a Greater Italy. The extinction of Fascism meant, for him, the end of his hopes for the future.

In American history, Robert E. Lee served the Confederate States of America during the Civil War of 1861–1865, even though he deplored slavery and opposed secession. Just so did Gentile serve Fascism. Both fought for what they conceived to be of more significance than personal prudence and of greater value than their immediate moral reservations.

There is really no satisfactory answer to questions of why such individuals remain loyal to political systems marred by moral failures. Why did not the Founding Fathers of the American Republic withdraw their support when the system, for which they had so long labored, institutionalized slavery—after they had all committed themselves to the moral conviction that "all men are created equal"? Why did not Nikolai Bukharin absent himself from the regime that had massacred untold numbers of innocents under Vladimir Lenin and Josef Stalin? And what of all the Chinese intellectuals who continued to support Mao Zedong after the madness of the "Great Leap Forward" and the massacre of perhaps millions in the "Great Proletarian Revolution"? And what of the countless Western intellectuals who found so much to admire in Stalinism and Maoism even after their respective barbarisms became common knowledge?

Such questions can be asked of intellectuals and theoreticians in any political system—and it is one that is legitimately addressed to Giovanni Gentile. But in asking the question, it is necessary to assess all intellectuals, everywhere, by the same moral criteria. Gentile, perhaps more than many of the others, had better answers.

Beyond all that, what is interesting for those of us at the turn of the new millenium, is the question of what "fascism" is understood to be, and have been. Identifying Fascism with Hitler's National Socialism, many academics have simply accepted the notion that generic fascism is the embodiment of evil and racism. As a consequence, they have been incapable of recognizing any of the real variants of Fascism when and where they appear.

Fascism saw itself as manifesting the righteous resistance of a newly emergent, less-developed nation, to the hegemonic, and imperialistic power of the industrialized nations of the West. From its very conception, Fascism opposed itself to those powers that had arrogated to themselves three-quarters of the earth's surface and almost all its resources. The Second World War, that saw its destruction, was a war that Fascists conceived as a war of redistribution—an occasion through which the "proletarian" nations of the world would finally "emerge into the sunlight."

These were the circumstances in which Gentile committed himself to Fascism. Like many Fascists, Gentile saw the twentieth century as a time of historic resolution. Italy, as a "proletarian" nation, would finally attain its proper station in the world. After a thousand years of oppression, invasion, and foreign rule, Italy would finally fulfill its "historic destiny."

Perhaps what is most interesting when all that is said, is to attempt some assessment of how understanding something of Fascism might help us to understand the last century—a time of unprecedented destruction of life and property. In that regard, arguments have been made and defended for more than a quarter of a century that contend that Fascism provided a model instance of revolution in the twentieth century.[15]

It was Fascism that identified the "mission" of revolution in the twentieth century—the attainment of a "place in the sun" for those nations that had "come late" to industrialization and modernization.[16] It was Fascism that characterized the institutionalization of the revolutionary state that would sustain the process: a single party dominance with hierarchical allocations of power. It was Fascism that exemplified the special features of the post-revolutionary state: the appearance of the charismatic leader, the "*duce*," the "*vohzd*," the "dear leader," the "*fuehrer*," the "*lider massimo*," the "chairman" who was the "never setting red sun." It was Fascism that was unremittingly statist and collectivist when less coherent revolutionaries were still anticipating the "withering away of the state" and the realization of anarcho-syndicalist rule.

It was Mussolini, and Fascist theorists, who early realized that Fascism would be more than a local phenomenon.[17] It was they who spoke of the shared authoritarianism, statism, elitism, anti-liberalism, and anti-parliamentarianism that characterized the anti-democratic revolutions of the "Left" and the "Right." They were among the first to dismiss the characterizations of Left and Right as having no cognitive or comparative merit. For all the talk of "class struggle" and "proletarian revolution" on the Left, Fascists insisted that the revolutions of the twentieth century would be "class struggles" only in the sense that the century would see "poor nations" and "young nations" engaging the "plutocracies" and "imperialist" powers in struggles for "living space" and resources.[18] Whether these systems claimed to be of the Left or Right, they would all eventually become irrepressibly nationalistic—whether they identified their nationalism as "patriotism" or racism.

Even the dynamic features of the several systems were shared. In all of them, workers, in general, were paid a standard low wage in order to underwrite what was variously called "primitive socialist accumulation" or "working for the Fatherland's future." In all such regimes, the "bureaucratic bourgeoisie" managed the system. Various forms of "corporativism" gradually emerged in all of them—and some form of "democratic centralism"[19] was all but universally characteristic.

Like all comparative categories, the several members of the class of "anti-democratic reactive developmental nationalisms" display marked differences. National Socialism was as different from Fascism as was Stalinism—and Stalinism was as different from Maoism as Maoism was from Castroism or the system of Kim Il Sung.

Perhaps the most significant difference turned on their respective inhumanity. Some were clearly genocidal or mass-murder regimes. Others were incarceration and exile regimes.[20] Fascism clearly fell into the latter category. Fascism, as almost everyone now acknowledges, was a "mild totalitarianism"—characterized by so little "terror" and so few political murders that many have simply refused to identify it as a "totalitarianism" at all.[21]

The "mildness" of Italian Fascism has been attributed to many things: Italian cultural and religious traditions, the "intrinsically humane" qualities of Latins—or their fundamental good sense. For all that, an argument can be made that Italians have shown themselves to be as homicidal and brutal as any. The barbarity of the civil war in Italy that preceded the March on Rome—and that which terminated the Second World War—might well have convinced everyone of that.[22]

Given such considerations, a plausible case might be made for the influence of Gentile's vision of Fascism as a moderating factor. His emphasis on the ethics of political behavior, together with his radical humanism, could only have given all men of conscience pause. At the end and in fact, that was precisely what aroused the venomous ire of his most intransigent opponents. Gentile was the conscience of Fascism—a conscience singularly missing from National Socialism, and Marxist-Leninist totalitarianisms.

All the totalitarianisms of the twentieth century were predicated on a systematic, anti-individualistic collectivism. In the case of Marxist-Leninism, the source was classical Marxism. Gentile had carefully dissected the neo-Hegelian roots of that collectivism. What he found missing in the collectivism of Marx was ethical concern. He sought to provide that concern to the collectivism of Fascism—a collectivism that shared a common intellectual origin with Marxism and Marxism-Leninism.[23]

At the beginning of the twenty-first century, those in the post-industrial democracies can anticipate an indeterminate period of difficulty with collectivistically oriented, anti-democratic, reactive nationalist, developmental, and single-party systems. Such systems will be found in Eastern Europe and the Balkans, in East and possibly Southeast Asia, and perhaps in Africa. People will be mobilized by questions of sovereign independence, international status, and irredentism. There will be talk of revolutionary resistance to the oppression of foreign imperialisms—and there will be calls to sacrificial commitment, to labor without compensation, and for a readiness to die for the community.[24] There will be talk of a place in the sun for those long humiliated and abused by the pretense and exploitation of foreigners.[25] Much of the talk will echo many of the themes of political Actualism. If that talk includes the appeals to moral responsibility that was at the center of Actualism, it may serve to moderate the passions of revolution—and we may be spared the genocide and mass murder of Nazism and Marxism-Leninism.

Notes

Abbreviations for Giovanni Gentile's
Works cited in the Endnotes

AP *L'Atto del pensare come atto puro* (Florence: Sansoni, 1937).
DP *Dottrina politica del fascismo* (Padua: CEDAM, 1937).
DR *Discorsi di religione* (Florence: Sansoni, 1955).
DV *Dopo la vittoria: Nuovi frammenti politici* (Rome: La Voce, 1920).
FA *La Filosofia dell'arte* (Milan: Treves, 1931).
FC *Fascismo e cultura* (Milan: Treves, 1928).
FD *I Fondamenti della filosofia del diritto* (Florence: Sansoni, 1955).
FI *La Filosofia italiana contemporanea: Due scritti* (Florence: Sansoni, 1955).
GS *Genesi e struttura della società: Saggio di filosofia pratica* (Florence: Sansoni, 1946).
IF *Introduzione alla filosofia* (Rome: Treves-Treccani-Tumminelli, 1932).
MI *Memorie italiane e problema della filosofia e della vita* (Florence: Sansoni, 1936).
MR *Il Modernismo e i rapporti fra religione e filosofia* (Florence: Sansoni, 1962).
OF *Le Origini della filosofia contemporanea in Italia* (Messina: Principato, 1923).
PS *Preliminari allo studio del fanciullo: Appunti* (Forence: Sansoni, 1922).
RD *La Riforma della dialettica hegeliano* (Florence: Sansoni, 1954).
RE *La Riforma dell'educazione: Discorsi ai maestri di Trieste* (Florence: Sansoni, 1955).
SL *Sistema di logica come teoria del conoscere* (Florence: Sansoni, 1940).
SP *Scritti pedagogici* (Milan: Treves-Treccani-Tumminelli, 1932).
SS *Sommario di pedagogia come scienza filosofica* (Florence: Sansoni, 1954).
TS *Teoria generale dello spirito come atto puro* (Bari: Laterza, 1924).

Chapter 1

1. The thesis was published in 1898 as *Rosmini e Gioberti* (and in a second edition in 1943. Florence: Sansoni, 1943). In his thesis, Gentile lamented that the major powers of Europe simply neglected the development of Italian philosophical thought. It is clear that for the young Gentile, Italy was treated as a negligible cultural factor. Beyond that, it was clear that both Gioberti and Rosmini were important Italian thinkers for Gentile. Gioberti had a substantial relationship with Giuseppe Mazzini, one of the major figures of Italy's Risorgimento—the unifica-

tion of Italy. Gentile maintained a continuous preoccupation with the thought of Mazzini, and the unification of Italy, throughout his life. See Gentile, *Albori della nuova Italia: varietà e documenti: Parte prima* (Lanciano: Carabba, 1923), pp. 233–237.

2. See "Bertrando Spaventa nel primo Cinquantenario della sua morte," *MI*, pp. 121–150.
3. "Adesione al Partito Fascista," in *SP*, 3, pp. 127–128.
4. Throughout the Fascist period, the government was referred to as "the regime." That practice will be continued here to distinguish the Fascist regime from other regimes.
5. See Gisella Longo, *L'Istituto nazionale fascista di cultura: Gli intellettuali tra partito e regime* (Rome: Pellicani, 2000).
6. In 1934, Gentile's works were placed on the Roman Catholic Index of proscribed literature.
7. See introduction to Benito Mussolini, "La dottrina del fascismo," *Scritti e discorsi* (Milan: Hoepli, 1934), 8, p. 67.
8. Nino Tripodi, *Il fascismo secondo Mussolini* (Rome: Il Borghese, 1971), p. 39.
9. Domenico Pellegrini-Giampietro, *Aspetti storici e spirituali del fascismo* (Rome: Vallerini, 1941), p. 103.
10. The Repubblica Sociale Italiano.

Chapter 2

1. For their translation, see Giovanni Gentile, *Origins and Doctrine of Fascism, Together with Selections from other of his Works* (New Brunswick, N.J.: Transaction, 2001. Translated by A. James Gregor).
2. *DV*, p. 85.
3. *DV*, p. 65.
4. See, for example, Napoleone Colajanni, *Latini e Anglo-Sassoni: Razze inferiori e razze superiori* (Rome: Rivista Populare, 1906); Sergi, *Decadenza delle nazioni latine* (Turin: Bocca, 1900); and the subsequent discussion in Roberto Michels, *Lavoro e razza* (Milan: Vallardi, 1924).
5. See the discussion in George Boas, *Dominant Themes of Modern Philosophy* (New York: Ronald Press, 1957), pp. 160–173.
6. See David Hume, *An Inquiry Concerning Human Understanding*, Section One, paras. 1–5.
7. "Dialectical Materialism" was largely the product of Friedrich Engels' interpretation of Marx's thought. "Historical Materialism" was essentially the work of Marx. It is not clear that the two materialisms were ever fully compatible. See A. James Gregor, *A Survey of Marxism: Problems in Philosophy and the Theory of History* (New York: Random House, 1965), pp. 45–55.
8. See the many editions of the works of Ardigò, *Opere filosofiche* (Padua: Il vero, 1891), together with Erminio Troilo, *Idee e ideali del positivismo* (Rome: Voghera, 1909) and *Il positivismo e i diritti dello spirito* (Turin: Bocca, 1912).
9. See *OF*, 2, chap. 1, and 3, parts 1 and 2.
10. *OF*, p. 4.
11. In this context, see Georgy Plekhanov, *The Development of the Monist View of History* in *Selected Philosophical Works* (Moscow: Foreign Languages, n.d.). The statement was the orthodox interpretation of classical Marxism that was then prevalent among the founders of Russian Marxism.

12. Hume, *An Enquiry Concerning Human Understanding*, Section XII, Part 1, para. 122.
13. See the discussion in I. M. Bochenski, *Contemporary European Philosophy* (Berkeley: University of California Press, 1956), pp. 12–15.
14. Ugo Spirito, *Il pragmatismo nella filosofia contemporanea: Saggio critico* (Florence: Vallecchi, 1921), pp. 131–132.
15. Ibid., pp. 167–179.
16. "Una critica del materialismo storico," in *FD*, pp. 131–196.
17. See for example, *FD*, pp. 175–176, 183–186.
18. See Gregor, *Survey of Marxism*, pp. 206–207.
19. All of this was given manifest expression in the germinal work of Georges Sorel, *Saggi di critica del Marxismo* (Milan: Sandron, 1903).
20. See Enzo Santarelli, *La revisione del marxismo in Italia* (Milan: Feltrinelli, 1977) and Irving Louis Horowitz, *Radicalism and the Revolt Against Reason: The Social Theories of Georges Sorel* (New York: Humanities Press, 1961). Gentile, at twenty-two, was eminently aware of these developments. He objected to the dominant positivism of the time. He referred to the work of the Darwinists, and Herbert Spencer—and then alluded to the work of Sorel as part of the general critique of materialism and determinism. See "La filosofia della prassi," *FD*, pp. 202, 231, 232, 238, 248, 251, 261, 265 n.1, 280.
21. One of the more characteristic expressions of these sentiments is to be found in Giovanni Papini and Giuseppe Prezzolini, *Vecchio e nuovo nazionalismo* (Rome: Volpe, 1967, reprint of the 1914 edition).
22. See the account in Spirito, *Il pragmatismo nella filosofia contemporanea*.
23. In this context, see the arguments of Italian Nationalists, particularly Enrico Corradini, *La Rinascita nazionale: Scritti raccolti e ordinati* (Florence: Felice le Monnier, 1929) and *Discorsi politici (1902–1923)* (Florence: Vallechi, 1923).
24. See the discussion of Benedetto Croce, *Storia d'Italia dal 1871 al 1915* (Bari: Laterza, 1928), pp. 250–259.
25. See Gioacchino Volpe, *Italia moderna 1898/1910* (Florence: Sansoni, 1973), 2, pp. 321–327.
26. Zeev Sternhell, *The Birth of Fascist Ideology* (Princeton: Princeton University Press, 1994), p. 33; A. James Gregor, *Young Mussolini and the Intellectual Origins of Fascism* (Berkeley: University of California Press, 1979), chaps. 1–3.
27. Benito Mussolini, "L'Uomo e la divinità," *Opera omnia* (Florence: La fenice, 1961–1974. Hereafter cited as *Oo*.), 33, pp. 5–37.
28. *Oo*, 33, pp. 6, 9, 11.
29. Mussolini, "'La Voce'" *Oo*, 2, p. 53.
30. See, for example, Mussolini, "Replica a Graziadei," *Oo*, 6, pp. 242–250.
31. See Gentile's discussion of the relationship of science to the nation's interests in 1923. "La moralità della scienza," *SP*, 3, pp. 61–79.
32. In 1898, with the publication of his thesis, *Rosmini e Gioberti: Saggio storico sulla filosofia Italiana del Risorgimento* (Florence: Sansoni, 1958, Third Edition), Gentile lamented that European thought allowed little, if any, place for Italian philosophy. "Foreigners," Gentile maintained, "were convinced that among Italians every vein of true philosophy had desiccated." Italy was understood as a negligible imitator of the thought of foreigners (pp. ix and x). It is evident that he dedicated his work to the restoration of a place for Italian thought as the equal of any in Europe.

Chapter 3

1. J. H. Stirling, *The Secret of Hegel* (Edinburgh: Oliver and Boyd, 1898); T. H. Green, *Prolegomena to Ethics* (Oxford: Clarendon, 1884); F. H. Bradley, *Appearance and Reality: A Metaphysical Essay* (London: Allen and Unwin, 1897).
2. A. J. Ayer, "Hume," in J. Dunn, J. O. Urmson and A. J. Ayer, *The British Empiricists* (New York: Oxford University Press, 1992), p. 200.
3. See L. de Broglie, *Matter and Light* (New York: W. W. Norton, 1939); Werner Heisenberg, *Physics and Philosophy* (New York: Harper, 1958).
4. See C. Joad, *Philosophical Aspects of Modern Science* (London: Allen and Unwin, 1948), pp. 20–21.
5. E. Schroedinger, *Science and Humanism* (Cambridge, Mass.: Harvard University Press, 1952), p. 24; see the introduction to Schroedinger, *Science, Theory and Man* (New York: Dover, 1957), p. xviii.
6. "Concezione umanistica del mondo," *IF*, pp. 1–19.
7. There are, of course, some very good works. Among the best is H. S. Harris, *The Social Philosophy of Giovanni Gentile* (Urbana: University of Illinois Press, 1960). Also available are Roger W. Holmes, *The Idealism of Giovanni Gentile* (New York: Macmillan, 1937); Patrick Romanell, *The Philosophy of Giovanni Gentile: An Inquiry into Gentile's Conception of Experience* (New York: Vanni, 1938); Aline Lion, *The Idealistic Conception of Religion* (Oxford: Clarendon Press, 1932); William A. Smith, *Giovanni Gentile on the Existence of God* (Paris: Beatrice-Nauwelaerts, 1970).
8. See A. James Gregor, *Phoenix: Fascism in Our Time* (New Brunswick, N. J.: Transaction, 1999), chap. 5.
9. See J. A. Smith, "The Philosophy of Giovanni Gentile," *Proceedings of the Aristotelian Society*, 20 (1919/1920), pp. 63–78; and H. W. Carr, "Translator's Introduction," Giovanni Gentile, *The Theory of Mind as Pure Act* (New York: Macmillan, 1922), pp. xi-xii.
10. See Lino Di Stefano, *La filosofia di G. Gentile* (Frosinone: Frusinate, 1974), p. 9.
11. Originally published in 1912 by the Biblioteca filosofica.
12. Bari: Laterza, 1924 (fourth edition). As indicated, the title is rendered *The Theory of Mind as Pure Act*. The Italian *"spirito"* is rendered "mind" in the title. It is not immediately evident that such a translation is apt, but the English term "spirit," with all its unfortunate connotations, certainly would not do.
13. *TS*, pp. 1–4.
14. *TS*, p. 3.
15. "O scetticismo o razionalismo," *MR*, p. 198.
16. Hume, *Enquiry Concerning Human Understanding*, Section XII, Part 1, para.119.
17. "Il regno dello spirito," *MR*, p. 238.
18. *GS*, p. 12.
19. *DR*, p. 24.
20. *AP*, p. 29–30.
21. *TS*, 236; see *DR*, p. 63.
22. *TS*, pp. 37–39. The notion originates in the work of Bertrando Spavento, *Scritti filosofici* (Naples: Morano, 1900), pp. 197–200; see *OF*, 3, part 2, pp. 140–184.
23. *SL*, 1940), 1, p. 46.
24. See *RE*, chap. 7.
25. See the discussion in "L'Esperienza," *IF*, pp. 88–115.
26. *SL*, 1, pp. 76–79.

27. In his opening address before the National Congress of Pure and Applied Chemistry, Gentile affirmed that "abstract" science is "directed toward a practical and concrete purpose," "La scienza e il paese," *SP*, p. 137.
28. See the entire discussion in Spirito, *Il pragmatismo nella filosofia contemporanea*.
29. See *SL*, 1, p. 151.
30. See the entire discussion in *SL*, part one, chapter 7, paras. 3–7, pp. 140–145.
31. *FA*, p. 304.
32. See the discussion in *DR*, pp. 52–53 and "Scienza e filosofia," *IF*, pp. 191–205.
33. *DR*, p. 40.
34. *DR*, p. 79.
35. Leo Lugarini, "Il problema della logica nella filosofia di Giovanni Gentile," *Giovanni Gentile: La vita e il pensiero* (Florence: Sansoni, 1954), 7, p. 145.
36. *GS*, p. 100.
37. See the discussion in *SL*, 2, Part 3, chap. 7.
38. *GS*, p. 44.
39. *GS*. See the formulation in "One can say: *be human!* To be human signifies to create oneself," in *SS*, 2, p. 44.
40. See *RE*, chaps. 5 and 7.
41. *TS*, chaps. 2 and 8.
42. See the discussion in Max Aebischer, *Der Einzelne und der Staat nach Giovanni Gentile* (Freiburg: Kanisiusdruckerei, 1954), pp. 25–34.
43. C. E. M. Joad provides the following definition of "solipsism": "Solipsism I take to be the belief that my mind, or my mental states, or, to avoid the necessity of postulating an *ego*, mental states of which there is experience, constitute the Universe," "Is Neo-Idealism Reducible to Solipsism?" Aristotelian Society (ed.), *Relativity, Logic and Mysticism* (London: William and Norgate, 1923), p. 129.
44. See Novello Papafava, *L'Idealismo assoluto: considerazioni* (Milan: Athena, n.d.), pp. 121–135.
45. See the account in F. C. S. Schiller, "Is Neo-Idealism Reducible to Solipsism," in *Relativity, Logic and Mysticism*, pp.145–147.
46. *TS*, p. 7.
47. See Harris, *The Social Philosophy of Giovanni Gentile*, p. 301.
48. *DR*, p. 73.
49. *GS*, p. 33.
50. See, for example, *RD*, pp. 69–97; particularly pp. 81–96.
51. See "Concetti fondamentali dell'attualismo," *IF*, pp. 35–36.
52. *GS*, pp. 38–39; see pp. 33–36.
53. See "Le due democrazie," *DV*, pp. 107–113.
54. See *GS*, chap. 4.
55. See Benedetto Croce, "Intorno all'idealismo attuale," *La Voce*, 13 November 1913, p. 4.
56. See the discussion in Evelyn Underhill, "Can the New Idealism Dispense With Mysticism?" in *Relativity, Logic and Mysticism*, pp. 148–150.
57. See the discussion in *TS*, pp. 229–230.
58. *DR*, p. 100.
59. *DR*, p. 230.
60. "Scienza e filosofia," *IF*, p. 194.
61. *TS*, p. 197.
62. *DR*, pp. 35, 39; see p. 24.
63. *DR*, p. 24.
64. *DR*, p. 39. See the discussion in Gentile, "Scienza e filosofia," *IF*, pp. 202–205.

65. *TS*, chap. 9.
66. "Scienza e filosofia," *IF*, pp. 190–192.
67. See the interesting discussion in Ugo Spirito, "L'Eredità dell'attualismo," *Giovanni Gentile* (Florence: Sansoni, 1969), pp. 197–200; and Gentile, "Dall'identità di scienza e filosofia a *La vita come ricerca*," in *IF*, pp. 279–292.
68.▪ See the discussion in *TS*, chaps. 3 and 8.
69. *GS*, p. 7.
70. *GS*, p. 7.
71. *RD*, p. 188.
72. See the discussion in *FD*, pp. 3–11 and chaps. 2 and 3.
73. For some time after the Second World War, Western intellectuals maintained that Actualism had impaired science in Italy—particularly the social sciences. See, for example, Victor A. Rapport, Stephen C. Cappannari and Leonard W. Moss, "Sociology in Italy," *American Sociological Review*, 22 (August 1957), pp. 441–447, and Leonore Lichnowsky, in Alfred Weber, *Einfuehrung in die Soziologie* (Munich: R. Piper, 1955), p. 494. Some held that because Fascism was influenced by Actualism, which was, anti-positivist, sociology was suppressed. M. Salvadori, *Las ciencias sociales del siglo XX en Italia* (Mexico D.F.: Ensaos sociologicos, n.d.), p. 9 and G. Guvitch and W. Moore, *La sociologie au XXe siecle* (Paris: P.U.F., 1947), 2, pp. 643–657. Actually, the Gentilean educational reforms in 1923 made possible the introduction of sociology as a required academic subject in the University of Padua, the Faculty of Political Science in Rome, and the Institute of Social Science in Florence. After 1928, sociology became obligatory in the School and Faculty of Statistics in Rome, Padua, Milan, Florence, Bologna, and then Palermo. See A. Povina, *Balance de la sociologia contemporanea* (Rome: Società italiana di sociologia, 1957), p. 71. In general, the relationship between Actualism and social science has been misrepresented. See M. D'Addio, "Brevi considerazioni sulla sociologia in Italia," *Sociologia*, 3 (1958), pp. 67–77. There is little evidence that Actualism had any negative influence on the development of science in Italy. See A. James Gregor and Michele Marotta, "Sociology in Italy," *The Sociological Quarterly*, 2, 3 (July 1961), pp. 215–221.
74. See *FD*, pp. 12–13, 48; *IF*, chap. 5.
75. *TS*, p. 222.

Chapter 4

1. The major article, and revision of the article, are now available in "Politica e filosofia," *DV*, pp. 188–216, dated August 1918, and "Il Problema politico," in *DR*, pp. 3–29, dated 14 March 1920.
2. *DR*, pp. 3, 7, 9; *DV*, pp. 197.
3. Gentile always capitalized "the State." That practice will be followed in any of the quotations directly attributable to him.
4. *DR*, pp. 9, 21; *DV*, pp. 208–210, 216
5. "Il significato della vittoria," *DV*, p. 5; *DR*, p. 21.
6. *DR*, p. 23.
7. "Le Due democrazie," *DV*, pp. 110–111; *DR*, pp. 5, 26.
8. *DR*, pp. 12–15, 20.
9. This was the standard argument found in Fascist apologetics. See Spampanato, "Regime del popolo," in *Democrazia fascista* (Rome: "Politica nuova, 1933), pp. 153–211. It is an argument found in all collectivist states, whether of the "Right" or "Left."

10. "Il Significato della vittorio," and "L'Esempio del governo," *DV*, pp. 5, 9, 71; *DR*, p. 7.
11. "Ammonimenti," *DV*, p. 51.
12. *DR*, pp. 24–25; "Ordine," *DV*, pp. 46–48.
13. See the discussion in "Stato e categorie," *DV*, p. 99.
14. "Liberalismo e liberali," *DV*, p. 172.
15. See "Le Due democrazie," *DV*, pp. 110–113.
16. Gentile advocated an overall increase in industrial productivity even at the expense of a decline in consumption. He sought labor discipline in order that Italy might produce enough so that its citizens would not have to emigrate to survive. That would entail a program of development. See "L'Esempio del governo" and "Ammonimenti," *DV*, pp. 52–53, 64–65.
17. See "La crisi morale," *DV*, pp. 85–86.
18. See Mussolini, "Dottrina del fascismo," *Oo*, 34, p. 132, n. 1 and Enzo Misefari, *Il Quadrumviro col frustino: Michele Bianchi* (Cosenza: Lerici, 1977), pp. 138–139.

Chapter 5

1. See Ugo Spirito, "Gentile e Marx," *Giovanni Gentile: La vita e il pensiero* (Florence: Sansoni, 1969), 1, pp. 313–334.
2. See, as a case in point, the discussion in Gennaro Sasso, *Le due Italie di Giovanni Gentile* (Bologna: Il Mulino, 1998), chap. 8.
3. See the discussion in Gregor, *A Survey of Marxism*, chap. 1.
4. V. I. Lenin, *The Teaching of Karl Marx* (New York: International, 1930), p. 45.
5. See the comments in A. Labriola, *Studio su Marx* (Naples: Voce, 1926), pp. 34–36; Rudolfo Mondolfo, *Il materialismo storico in Federico Engels* (Genoa: Humanitas, 1912), pp. 9, 11; Sidney Hook, *Towards the Understanding of Karl Marx* (New York: Random House, 1933), p. 29; Max Adler, *Marx als Denker* (Berlin: Dumblot, 1925), pp. 126–141.
6. Karl Marx, "Theses on Feuerbach," *The German Ideology* (New York: International, 1988), pp. 120–123.
7. "La filosofia di Marx," *FD*, p. 214. For a more exhaustive treatment of this material, see A. James Gregor, "Giovanni Gentile and the Philosophy of the Young Karl Marx," *Journal of the History of Ideas*, 24, 2 (1963), pp. 213–230.
8. *FI*, pp. 41–42; see also *DR*, p. 24.
9. Karl Marx, *Economic and Philosophic Manuscripts of 1844* (Moscow: Foreign Languages, n.d.), p. 160; compare with Marx, *Die Fruehschriften* (Stuttgart: Echt, 1953), p. 277.
10. Ibid.
11. See the discussion in "La filosofia di Marx," *FD*, p. 207, n. 1. "Subjects and objects do not come together to create human activity: they are ever changing distinctions within it." Sidney Hook, *From Hegel to Marx* (New York: Humanities Press, 1950), p. 259.
12. Marx, *Economic and Philosophic Manuscripts of 1844* in Karl Marx, Frederick Engels, *Collected Works* (New York: International Publishers, 1976), 3, pp. 336, 337.
13. "La filosofia di Marx," *FD*, pp. 294–295, see p. 216; cf. J. Calvez, *La pensee de Karl Marx* (Paris: Editions du Seuil, 1956), pp. 383–385.
14. "La filosofia di Marx," *FD*, pp. 256, 298.
15. "This subject, without its object, of what is it a subject? And this object without

its respective subject, to whom is it an object?....Marx objects that the materialists...conceive the subject and the object of consciousness in an abstraction, and thereby falsely." *FD*, pp. 214, 216.

16. *FD*, p. 215.
17. *FD*, p. 225.
18. The whole discussion devoted to Hegel's *Phenomenology* is part of that effort. See Marx, *Economic and Philosophic Manuscripts of 1844*, pp. 330–346.
19. Ludwig Feuerbach, "Zur Kritik der Hegel'schen Philosophie," *Saemtliche Werke* (Leipzig: Otto Wigand, 1846), 2, pp. 252–253.
20. *FD*, pp. 301–303.
21. *FD*, p. 295.
22. See the discussion in "Politica e filosofia," *DV*, pp. 190–191.
23. *FD*, p. 215
24. See the comments in *FD*, pp. 221–222, 229–230.
25. There was a curious transposition of roles on the part of Marx and Engels in the course of their life-long collaboration. At the commencement of their labor, it was Marx, who was a trained philosopher, who wrote about epistemological and ontological subjects. Towards the end of Marx's life, Engels assumed the obligations of addressing such issues. Engels had been trained in economics, not philosophy. His writings clearly provide evidence of his lack of sophistication in either epistemology or ontology. See Gregor, *A Survey of Marxism*, chaps. 2 and 3.
26. Friedrich Engels, *Ludwig Feuerbach and the End of Classical Germany Philosophy*, in Karl Marx and Friedrich Engels, *Selected Works* (Moscow: Foreign Languages 1955), 2, p. 362, "Socialism: Utopian and Scientific," ibid., p. 100; *Dialectics of Nature* (Moscow: Foreign Languages, 1954), pp. 271, 280, 285.
27. Engels, *Anti-Duehring: Herr Eugen Duehring's Revolution in Science* (Moscow: Foreign Languages, 1962), p. 55; *Lugwig Feuerbach*, p. 362.
28. Engels, *Anti-Duehring*, p. 55.
29. Engels, "Socialism: Utopian and Scientific," Marx and Engels, *Selected Works*, pp. 100–101.
30. V. I. Lenin, *Materialism and Empirio-Criticism* (Moscow: Foreign Languages, 1947), pp. 104–106; see R. Garaudy, *Contribution a la Theorie Materialiste de la Connaissance* (Paris: PUF, 1954), p. 1; G. Wetter, *Der dialektische Materialismus* (Vienna: Herder, 1952), p. 515. For a more exhaustive treatment of this material see A. James Gregor, "Lenin on the Nature of Sensations," *Studies on the Left*, 3, 2 (1963), PP. 34–42.
31. See, for example, Hobbes, *Leviathan*, 1, para. i, and *De Corpore*, 1, para. vi, p. 10. Cf. F. Brandt, *Thomas Hobbes' Mechanical Conception of Nature* (Copenhagen: Levin, Munksgarrd, 1928), pp. 13–16.
32. H. Helmholtz, as cited in F. Erdmann, *Die philosopischen Grundlagen von Helmholtz' Wahrnemungstheorie* (Berlin: Akademie der Wissenschafter, 1921), p. 38.
33. Lenin, *Materialism and Empiriocriticism*, p. 237.
34. "The primary stage, the first step in the cognizance of any object—the simplest as well as the most complex—is in sense experience, our perceptions," M. Rosenthal, *Was ist marxistische Erkenntnistheorie?* (Berlin: Dietz, 1956), p. 27. "The question concerning the relationship between sense image (*Abbild*) and object is the fundamental question of the materialist theory of reflection (*Widerspiegelungstheorie*)," F. Chassachatschich, *Materie und Bewusstsein* (Berlin: Dietz, 1957), p. 133.
35. Gentile rejected the notion of conscious experience as somehow the "mirror or form or model of empirical reality." *FI*, p. 42.

36. Engels, in his later writings could maintain that "atoms and molecules, etc., cannot be observed under the microscope, but only by a process of thought." Friedrich Engels, *Dialectics of Nature* (New York: International, 1940), p. 154. Whatever the developments in electronmicroscopes, the epistemological problem remains—and the notion that we "perceive" imperceptibles in "thought" reveals the kind of problems that attend Marxism as epistemology.

37. Lenin, *Materialism and Empiriocriticism*, p. 267. Gentile had written long before that any effort to treat "matter" as a mind-independent something would leave it entirely without any properties whatever. "To think of matter by itself is to think a pure indeterminateness...." *TS*, p. 55.

38. Max Adler, *Lehrbuch der Materialistischen Geschichtsauffassung* (Berlin: Laubsche, 1930), 1, p. 120.

39. *FD*, p. 296.

40. *FD*, pp. 301–302.

41. *FD*, pp. 249–250.

42. Gentile defines as "metaphysical" any philosophy that is "intellectualistic," that is to say, presupposes a world independent and outside of mind, and possesses an "abstract" conception of history, seen as independent of human creativity and will. "Politica e filosofia," *DV*, p. 213.

43. Engels, *Anti-Duehring*, pp. 93, 515; *Dialectics of Nature*, pp. 93, 325, 337.

44. This explains the confidence some Leninists displayed in the conviction that the Marxist notion of "materialism" is "absolute" and "eternal." See V. Stern, *Zu einigen Fragen der marxistischen Philosophie* (Berlin: Aufbau, 1954), p. 41.

45. See the more extensive discussion in Gregor, *A Survey of Marxism*, chaps. 2 and 3.

46. See the entire discussion in *RE*, chaps. 4 and 7.

47. Karl Marx and Friedrich Engels, *The German Ideology* (New York: International, 1988), p. 42.

48. Ibid., p. 43.

49. Ibid., p. 47. Thus, "religion, family, state, law, morality, science art, etc., are only *particular* modes of poduction, and fall under its general law." Marx, *The Economic and Philosophic Manuscripts of 1844*, p. 297.

50. Karl Marx and Friedrich Engels, *Manifesto of the Communist Party* (Beijing: Foreign Languages, 1990), p. 49.

51. Marx and Engels, *The German Ideology*, p. 58.

52. See Manfred Buhr and Alfred Kosing, *Kleines Woerterbuch der marxistisch-leninistischen Philosophie* (Berlin: Dietz, 1966), pp. 52–53.

53. Georg Klaus and Manfred Buhr, "Ethik," *Philosophisches Woerterbuch* (Leipzig: VEB, 1966), p. 176.

54. See, for example, William Ash, *Marxism and Moral Concepts* (New York: Monthly Review, 1964), pp. 4–5.

55. V. I. Lenin, "The Economic Content of Narodism and the Criticism of It in Mr. Struve's Book," *Collected Works*, 1, pp. 420–421.

56. Among orthodox Marxists, one of the better books available is Karl Kautsky, *Ethik und materialistische Geschichtsauffassung* (Stuttgart: Dietz, 1919). Others, from the tradition of the Second International, sought to supplement Marxism with Kantian ethics.

57. As cited, Stefan Vogovic, *L'Etica comunista* (Rome: Citta Nuova, 1966), p. 139.

58. See the entire discussion in Leon Trotsky, *Terrorism and Communism* (Ann Arbor: University of Michigan, 1961).

59. A. F. Schischkin, *Grundlagen der marxistischen Ethik* (Berlin: Dietz, 1964), pp. 48–49.

60. Ibid., pp. 53, 530–531.
61. *FD*, pp. 196, 202.
62. See the discussion in Spirito, "Gentile e Marx," *Giovanni Gentile*, particularly pp. 331–334.
63. *FD*, p. vii.

Chapter 6

1. See the account in Gabriele Turi, *Giovanni Gentile: Una biografia* (Florence: Giunti, 1995), pp. 40–43.
2. See the discussion in G. De Ruggiero, *La filosofia contemporanea* (Bari: Laterza, 1912), pp. 358, 432; and Turi, *Giovanni Gentile*, pp. 207–208.
3. See the discussion in Herve A. Cavallera, *Reflessione e azione formativa: l'Attualismo di Giovanni Gentile* (Rome: Fondazione Ugo Spirito, 1996), pp. 35–43, and chap. 3.
4. See Paolo Ungari, *Alfredo Rocco e l'ideologia giuridica del fascismo* (Brescia: Morcelliana, 1963).
5. In 1913, Mussolini, while still a revolutionary socialist, could speak of "the crisis of the positivistic philosophical systems...." Mussolini, "Al largo!" *Oo*, 6, p. 5.
6. Emilio Gentile, *Mussolini & La Voce* (Florence: Sansoni, 1976), p. 2; see the reproduction of the announcement of the publication of *La Voce* in Giuseppe Prezzolini, *Il tempo della Voce* (Milan: Vallecchi, 1960), facing p. 16.
7. Turi, *Giovanni Gentile*, p. 316.
8. *GS*, chap. 5.
9. *FD*, pp. 228, 229.
10. *FD*, pp. 212, 226–229.
11. Marx, "On the Jewish Question," in Karl Marx and Friedrich Engels, *Collected Works* (New York: International, 1971–1976. Hereafter cited as *MECW*), 3, p. 164.
12. Ibid., p. 173.
13. Ibid., p. 164.
14. Ibid.
15. See A. F. Schischkin, *Grundlagen der marxistischen Ethik* (Berlin: Dietz, 1964), pp. 238, 242.
16. "Liberalismo e liberali," *DV*, p. 172.
17. "Le due democrazie," *DV*, pp. 110, 111.
18. "L'Idea monarchica," *DV*, p. 154.
19. These same ideas remained constant in Gentile's exposition. See *GS*, p. 13.
20. "Il problema politico," *DR*, p. 21.
21. See the later discussion in "Lo Stato e la filosofia," *IF*, pp. 179–180.
22. *GS*, pp.14,15.
23. *GS*, p. 44.
24. Years later, in 1932, these conceptions appeared in the first section of the *Dottrina del fascismo*.
25. See the entire discussion in Marx's "On the Jewish Question," *MECW*, 3, pp. 146–174.
26. Marx and Engels, "Manifesto of the Communist Party," *MECW*, 6, p. 503.
27. Ibid., pp. 512, 514, 515.
28. Engels, "Principles of Communism," *MECW*, 3, p. 349.
29. See the more ample discussion in Gregor, *Survey of Marxism*, pp. 175–185.

30. *DV*, p. 216.
31. This is the central argument of Actualism. Each domain is given special treatment, but all ultimately rest on the commonality, the "universality" of thinking as "pure act." See the special discussions in *FAC*, and "Il sentimento," "L'arte," "Arte e religione, "Scienza e filosofia," and "Nuova dimostrazione dell'esistenza di Dio," in *IF*.
32. See the account in *PS*.
33. A synoptic version of the entire argument is found in English in H. S. Harris' translation of Gentile's *Genesis and Structure of Society* (Urbana: University of Illinois Press, 1960).
34. For a more ample discussion, see Gregor, *Young Mussolini and the Intellectual Origins of Fascism* and *The Ideology of Fascism: The Rationale of Totalitarianism* (New York: Free Press, 1969) chaps. 1–4.
35. See the efforts by the orthodox Marxist, Georgy Plekhanov, to solve these issues in Plekhanov, *The Role of the Individual in History* (New York: International Publishers, n.d.).
36. Mussolini, "Al largo!" *Oo*, 6, p. 7.
37. Mussolini, "Replica a Graziadei," *Oo*, 6, p. 249.
38. See Mussolini's discussion in the "Dottrina politica e sociale," to be found in *La dottrina del fascismo* in *Oo*, 34, 122–123 and "La teoria sindacalista," *Oo*, 2, pp. 123–128.
39. Mussolini suggested that the ideas of Gentile might have influenced him as early as 1908. Yvon De Begnac, *Palazzo Venezia: Storia di un regime* (Rome: La Rocca, 1950), p. 133.
40. See the discussion in Gregor, *Ideology of Fascism*, pp. 102–103.
41. See Mussolini, "'La Voce,'" *Oo*, 2, pp. 53–56.
42. See the contemporary comments by Scipio Slataper in Giuseppe Prezzolini, *Il tempo della Voce* (Rome: Longanesi, 1960), p. 397.
43. See the discussion in Gregor, *Phoenix*, chap. 2.
44. See Mussolini's account, years later, in Mussolini, "Il governo fascista e la nazione," *Oo*, 21, pp. 97–98.
45. See Gregor, *Ideology of Fascism*, chaps. 2, 3.
46. See the comments in Gentile, *Le origini dell'ideologia fascista*, p. 327.
47. The majority of Gentile's publications originating in this period are collected in *Guerra e fede: Frammenti politici* (Naples: Ricciardi, 1919) and *DV*.
48. See the discussion in "Il significato della vittoria," *DV*, pp. 3–25.
49. "La crisi morale," *DV*, p. 85.
50. "Le due democrazie," *DV*, pp. 111, 112.
51. "Liberalismo e liberale," *DV*, p. 172.
52. "Il problema politico," *DR*, p. 21.
53. "Il problema politico," *DR*, p. 7.
54. "L'Epilogo," *DV*, pp. 27, 51; see "L'Esempio del governo," *DR*, pp. 64–65.
55. "Il problema politico," *DR*, p. 9.
56. See the discussion in "Il significato della vittoria," *DV*, pp. 5–8.
57. See the discussion in *SL*, 2, chap. 6.
58. Years later, Gentile was to express these convictions in *GS*, p. 162 and still more expressly in *DP*.
59. This is a summary rendering of discussions to be found in *FD*, chaps. 2 and 4, *IF*, chap. 6.
60. These themes run throughout Gentile's pedagogical works.
61. See Gentile's discussion in "Contro l'agnosticismo della scuola," *FC*, pp. 38–43.

62. Turi, *Giovanni Gentile*, p. 241.
63. Mussolini, "La culla e il resto," *Oo*, 17, p. 90; "Deviazioni," *Oo*, 17, p. 129.
64. Mussolini, "Da che parte va il mondo? *Oo*, 18, p. 70.
65. Mussolini, "Per la vera pacificazione," *Oo*, 18, p. 298.
66. Mussolini, "L'Avvenimento," *Oo*, p. 127,
67. Mussolini, "L'Italia e la triplice," *Oo*, 6, p. 329.
68. Gentile consistently spoke of his idealism as a "religious movement." See "Il carattere religioso dell'idealismo italiano," *MI*, pp. 323–340.
69. Mussolini, "Per la vera pacificazione," *Oo*, p. 292.
70. Mussolini, "Il programma fascista," *Oo*, p. 220.
71. Gentile, *Le origini dell'ideologia fascista*, 348; Turi, *Giovanni Gentile*, p. 307.
72. "Manifesto degl'intellettuali italiani fascisti agli intellettuali di tutte le nazioni," in Gentile, *Le origini dell'ideologia fascista*, pp. 459–466.
73. Mussolini, "Il primo discorso all camera dei deputati," *Oo*, 16, p. 445. In the Fall of 1921, he repeated the same notions. Mussolini, "Il fascismo e già un partito," *Oo*, 17, p. 158.
74. Mussolini, "Programma e statuti del partito nazionale fascista," *Oo*, 17, p. 335.
75. See, for example, Mussolini, "Al popolo dell'Aquila," *Oo*, 21, pp. 112–113.
76. See Turi, *Giovanni Gentile*, pp. 337–339.
77. Mussolini, "Discorso del 3 Gennaio," *Oo*, 21, pp. 235–241.
78. Mussolini, "Intransigenza assoluta," *Oo*, 21, pp. 362, 363.
79. See Mussolini, "All'Assemblea quinquennale del regime," *Oo*, 24, pp. 15–16.
80. See, for example, the discussion in Gherardo Casini, "Classici, romantici e scettici del pensiero fascista," *La Rivoluzione fascista*, 18 May 1924, and "Volt," "Le cinque anime del fascismo," *Critica fascista*, 15 February 1925, both reproduced in Gentile, *Le origini dell'ideologia fascista*, pp. 448–459.
81. Mussolini, "Per la medaglia dei benemeriti del comune di Milano," *Oo*, 21, p. 425.
82. Mussolini, "La dottrina del fascismo," *Oo*, 34, pp. 117–138.
83. See the discussion in Gregor, *Phoenix*, chap. 6.
84. Mussolini, "Dottrina del fascismo," *Oo*, 34, pp. 117–121.
85. "Le due democrazie," *DV*, p.
86. See Renzo De Felice, *Mussolini il duce: Gli anni del consenso 1929–1936* (Turin: Einaudi, 1974).
87. See the entire rationale in *DP* and the acknowledgment in Turi, *Giovanni Gentile*, pp. 407–412.

Chapter 7

1. See "Il carattere religioso dell'idealismo italiano," "La nuova università italiana e il problema dei giovani," and "L'Ideale della cultura e l'Italia presente," *MI*, pp. 323–385.
2. *FC*, pp. 74–75.
3. See, for example, Luisa Mangoni, *L'Interventismo della cultura: Intellettuali e riviste del fascismo* (Bari: Laterza, 1974).
4. See the entire discussion in Francois Furet, *The Passing of an Illusion: The Idea of Communism in the Twentieth Cetnury* (Chicago: University of Chicago Press, 1999), particularly p. 482.
5. See Stephane Courtois, Nicolas Werth, Jean-Louis Penne, Andrzej Paczkowski, Karel Bartosek, and Jean-Louis Margolin, *The Black Book of Communism: Crimes,*

Terror, Repression (Cambridge, Mass.: Harvard University Press, 1999), chap. 10, pp. 289–319.

6. See the discussion in Turi, *Giovanni Gentile*, pp. 419–420.

7. P. Angelo Zacchi, *Il nuovo idealism italiano di B. Croce e G. Gentile* (Rome: Ferrari, 1925), pp. 281–292.

8. See the work by Armando Carlini, a long-time Actualist, that sought to distinguish Mussolini's thought from that of Gentile.

9. Armando Carlini, *Filosofia e religione nel pensiero di Mussolini* (Rome: Istituto nazionale fascista di cultura, 1934).

10. Ibid., pp. 13–15, 19.

11. Years after Gentile's death, Carlini repeated essentially the same account. See Carlini, "Il pensiero politico di G. Gentile," in *Giovanni Gentile*, 8, pp. 115–118.

12. Ibid., p. 31.

13. Mussolini, "All'Assemblea quinquennale del Regime," *Oo*, 24, pp. 15–16.

14. Carlini, *Filosofia e religione nel pensiero di Mussolini*, pp. 33–35.

15. Ibid., p. 36.

16. Ibid., pp. 31, 38

17. *FC*, p. 175. See Gentile's efforts to deal with the issue of religion and the state's responsibilities with regard to the moral and spiritual training of Fascists. *CF*, pp. 103–106; *IF*, pp. 184–187; *FC*, pp. 67–75, 92–115, 122–145, 146–181.

18. Gentile, *La mia religione* (Florence: Sansoni, 1943), pp. 6–7; see Ugo Spirito, "La religione de Giovanni Gentile," *Giovanni Gentile*, 7, pp. 321–333. The resolution for Gentile rested in the fact that his Actualism accommodated both Fascism and Roman Catholicism by making Catholicism *immanent* in thought. Again, it seems that there was no place for a transcendent God in his system.

19. G. Silvano Spinetti, *Fascismo e libertà (Verso una nuova sintesi)* (Padua: CEDAM, 1941), p. 115; see chap. 8.

20. See the discussion in Ferruccio Pardo, *La filosofia di Giovanni Gentile: Genesi, sviluppo, unità sistematica, critica* (Florence: Sansoni, 1972), pp. 327–329.

21. See, for example, *CF*, p. 104.

22. Turi, *Giovanni Gentile*, p. 467.

23. Carlo Costamagna, *Dottrina del fascismo* (Turin: UTET, 1940), pp. 9, 31, 33, 149–150.

24. See the entire discussion in *GS*, chap. 6.

25. Costamagna, *Dottrina del fascismo*, pp. 23–24; see p. 19.

26. Ibid., pp. 148–150.

27. Ibid., p. 341.

28. Ibid., p. 161.

29. John Strachey Barnes, *The Universal Aspects of Fascism* (London: Williams and Norgate, 1929), pp. 94–95.

30. Sergio Panunzio, *Teoria generale dello stato fascista* (Padua: CEDAM, 1939), p. 5 and pp. 21–22.

31. Ibid., p. 22, n. 1.

32. Spinetti, in the pursuit of his ends, even objected to the anti-individualism of Alfredo Rocco and Sergio Panunzio—which suggests that he was prepared to abandon much of Fascism in order to defend the "divine essence" of the individual and the sovereignty of the Catholic Church. Spinetti, *Fascismo e libertà*, p. 100, n. 14.

33. Guido Cavallucci, *Il fascismo e sulla via di Mosca?* (Rome: Cremonese, 1933), pp. 16, 25, n. 8, 30.

34. Mussolini, "Per l'istituto mobiliare italiano," *Oo*, 25, pp. 64–65.

35. Mussolini, "Discorso per lo stato corporativo," *Oo*, 26, p. 87.
36. See the entire discussion in Salvatore Gatti, "Dalla concezione individualistica alla concezione fascista della proprietà privata," together with the series of articles contained in *La concezione fascista della proprietà privata* (Rome: Confederazione fascista dei laboratori dell'agricoltura, 1939), p. 17 and *passim*.
37. Ibid., pp. 12–13, 15–16.
38. Ibid., pp. 30, 31, n. 3, 39, 40.
39. Ibid., p. 32.
40. See Ugo Spirito, *Capitalismo e corporativismo* (Florence: Sansoni, 1933) and Spampanato, *Democrazia fascista*.
41. Spampanato, *Democrazia fascista*, pp. 218–219.
42. Mussolini, "Storia di un anno," *Oo*, 34, p. 410.
43. See Attilio Tamaro, *Venti anni di storia: Storia e documenti del fascismo* (Rome: Volpe, 1975), 3, pp. 78–80.
44. See Antonio Canepa, *Sistema di dottrina del fascismo* (Rome: Formiggini, 1937), 3, pp. 121–124. See Gentile's acknowledgment of criticism from Fascists. *FI*, pp. 8–12.
45. The neo-Hegelianism of Benedetto Croce clearly could not serve. Croce was a major anti-Fascist throughout much of the regime.
46. See Sasso, *Le due Italie di Giovanni Gentile*, p. 320, n. 7.

Chapter 8

1. See the discussion in Carlo De Biase, *L'Impero di "Faccetta Nera"* (Rome: "Il Borghese," 1966); C. Terracciano, G. Rolleto, and E. Masi (eds.), *Geopolitica fascista, antologia di scritti* (Milano: Barbarossa, 1993); Vito Beltani, *Il problema delle materie prime* (Rome: Tupini, 1940).
2. See Robert Mallett, *The Italian Navy and Fascist Expansionism 1935–1940* (London: Frank Cass, 1998), particularly chap. 2.
3. See the discussion in A. James Gregor, *A Place in the Sun* (Boulder, Colo.: Westview Press, 2000), chap. 8.
4. Galeazzo Ciano, *Ciano's Hidden Diary 1937–1938* (New York: Dutton, 1953), pp. 28–29.
5. See Mussolini's comments, entries of 8 January and 30 July, 1938 in Ciano, *Ciano's Hidden Diary 1937–1938*, pp. 62, 141, and Renzo De Felice, *Storia degli ebrei italiani sotto il fascismo* (Turin: Einaudi, 1993), pp. 237–238, n. 1.
6. De Felice, *Storia degli ebrei italiani sotto il fascismo*, p. 235.
7. See Mussolini's comments on 3 December 1937, p. 40; 6 February, and 13 February 1938, in *Ciano's Hidden Diary 1937–1938*, pp. 40, 71, 74.
8. Together with the study by De Felice, *Storia degli ebrei italiani sotto il fascismo*, and his account in *Mussolini il duce: Lo Stato totalitario* (Turin: Einaudi, 1996), chap. 3, the account by Meir Michaelis, *Mussolini and the Jews* (London: The Clarendon Press, 1978), together with Andrew M. Canepa, "Half-Hearted Cynicism: Mussolini's Racial Politics," *Patterns of Prejudice* 13, 6 (November-December 1979), pp. 18–27, is instructive.
9. For an English translation, see Gregor, *Ideology of Fascism*, Appendix A, pp. 383–386.
10. Editorial, "Politica fascista della razza," *Critica fascista*, 16, 19 (1 August 1938), pp. 290–291.
11. See Nicola Caracciolo, *Gli ebrei e l'Italia durante la guerra 1940–45* (Rome: Bonacci, 1986), pp. 17–30.

12. De Felice, *Storia degli ebrei italiani sotto il fascismo*, pp. 64–108; see the discussion in Dino Sanzo, *Il fascismo e gli ebrei* (Rome: Trevi, 1973).

13. See Luciano Elmo, *La condizione giuridica degli ebrei in Italia* (Milan: Baldini & Castoldi, 1939).

14. See Gentile's very early objections, in 1916, to those who proposed to use race as a determinant of human behavior. *TS*, p. 171.

15. Until the late 1930s, Mussolini had regularly argued against "Nordicism," or biological racism of any sort. See Gregor, *The Ideology of Fascism*, chap. 6.

16. See Giordano Bruno Guerri, *Il Giornale* (Milan), 7 March 2000, p. 7.

17. Bruno Brunello, a student of Gentile, in a review of a book on "Fascist" racism, identified it, in Gentile's *Giornale critico della filosofia italiana*, 18 (1937), pp. 202–205, as "a most flagrant negation of historicistic immanentism."

18. Balbino Giuliano, *Elementi di cultura fascista* (Bologna: Zanichelli, 1929), p. 120.

19. See H. W. Carr's "Translator's Introduction" to Giovanni Gentile, *The Theory of Mind as Pure Act* (New York: Macmillan, 1922) and R. G. Collingwood, "Can the New Idealism Dispense with Mysticism?" *Relativity, Logic, and Mysticism*, p. 165.

20. See the entire discussion in Gregor, *Ideology of Fascism*, chap. 6.

21. De Felice, *Storia degli ebrei italiani sotto il fascismo*, pp. 402–416; Giorgio Pisano, *Mussolini e gli ebrei* (Milan: FPE, 1970).

22. See Turi, *Giovanni Gentile*, p. 478.

23. Turi, ibid, pp. 476–477.

24. Paolo Conti, "L'Enciclopedia riapre il caso Gentile," *Corriere della sera* (Milan), 2 February 2000, p. 18.

25. Antonio Socci, "Gentile aiuto i prof ebrei fuggiti all'estero," *Il Giornale* (Milan), 10 September 1999, p. 6.

26. See the account in Benedetto Gentile in *Giovanni Gentile dal discorso agli italiani alla morte, 24 giugno 1943–15 aprile 1944* (Florence: Sansoni, 1951), p. 12.

27. Gentile, "Discorso agli italiani," in ibid., pp. 67–81.

28. See Alessandro Campi, "Giovanni Gentile," in Fabio Andriola (ed.), *Uomini e scelte della RSI: I protagonisti della Repubblica di Mussolini* (Foggia: Bastogi Editrice Italiana, 2000), pp. 21–41.

29. Gentile, "Recostruire," *Giovanni Gentile dal discorso agli Italiani alla morte*, pp. 86–87.

30. Attilio Tamaro, *Venti anni di storia* (Rome: Volpe, 1971), 2, p. 220.

31. See Carlo Mazzantini, *I balilla andarono a Salò* (Venice: Marsilio, 1995), pp. 105–113.

32. See Guglielmo Salotti, *Nicola Bombacci da Mosca a Salò* (Rome: Bonacci, 1986); Guglielmo Salotti, "Nicola Bombacci," in Andriola, *Uomini e scelte della RSI*, pp. 235–245.

33. De Felice, *Mussolini l'alleato: La guerra civile 1943–1945* (Turin: Einaudi, 1997), p. 539, n. 6, and pp. 539–544; Gloria Gabrielli, "Carlo Silvestri," in Andriola, *Uomini e scelte della RSI*, pp. 115–128.

34. See F. W. Deakin, *The Brutal Friendship: Mussolini, Hitler and the Fall of Italian Fascism* (New York: Harper and Row, 1962), p. 564 and Part 3, Book 1, chap. one.

35. De Felice, *Storia degli ebrei sotto il fascismo*, 454–458.

36. Ibid.; Deakin, *Brutal Friendship*, pp. 620–623.

37. It is estimated that Republican Fascists were complicit in the death of about seven thousand Italian Jews at the hands of German forces in Italy during 1943 and the end of the war. See Caracciolo, *Gli ebrei e l'Italia durante la guerra 1940–45*, pp. 29–30.

38. See Gentile, "Questione morale," "L'Accademia d'Italia e l'Italia di Mussolini," in *Giovanni Gentile dal discorso agli Italiani alla morte*, pp. 98–99, 101–103.
39. Gentile, "Giambattista Vico nel secondo centenario della morte," ibid., p. 115.
40. Carlo Costamagna (editor), "Professori ebrei e dottrina ebraica," *Lo Stato*, August-September 1938, p. 490.
41. See H. S. Harris, *The Social Philosophy of Giovanni Gentile*, p. 245, n. 3.
42. Immediately before his death, in his commemorative lecture before the *Accademia d'Italia*, Gentile had argued that the issue of a *transcendent* deity and a universal *immanence* was not one that could deny the Catholicism of a believer. Catholic authorities, for whatever reason, allowed his interment in hallowed ground. See Gentile, "Giambattista Vico...," *Giovanni Gentile dal discoro agli italiani alla morte*, p. 119.

Chapter 9

1. "It is doubtful if there is a more influential teacher in the intellectual world today." E. W. Carr "Introduction," Gentile, *The Theory of Mind as Pure Act*, p. xix.
2. See the discussion in Gregor, *Phoenix*, chap. 2.
3. Enrico Corradini, "Un biglietto sull'espansionismo," *Il Regno*, 1, 4 (1903), p. 24.
4. See G. Prezzolini, "Le due Italie," *Il Regno*, 1, 26 (1904), pp. 3–4; Prezzolini and Papini, *Vecchio e nuovo nazionalismo* (Rome: Volpe, 1967, republished from the 1914 edition).
5. M. Maraviglia, "Nazionalismo e democrazia," *Idea nazionale*, 14 December 1911.
6. Rocco, *Scritti e discorsi politici*, 1, p. 98.
7. See, in this context, Marialuisa Cicalese, *La formazione del pensiero politico di Giovanni Gentile (1896–1919)* (Milan: Marzorati, 1972), and Gregor, *Phoenix*, chaps. 1 and 2.
8. See A. James Gregor, *Italian Fascism and Developmental Dictatorship* (Princeton: Princeton University Press, 1979), chaps. 3 and 4.
9. *GS*, p. 44.
10. Mussolini, "L'uomo e la divinità," *Oo*, 33, p. 22.
11. See, for example, Harris, *The Social Philosophy of Giovanni Gentile*, pp. 185, 188; De Begnac, *Palazzo Venezia*, p. 641.
12. "Gentile, as Del Noce has explained, was the philosopher of Fascism. He provided the historical-philosophical core of Mussolini's movement, establishing its continuity with the history of Italy." Alessandro Campi, "Perchè Gentile doveva essere ucciso," *Il Giornale* (Milan), 24 January 2000, p. 3. "Gentile provided the regime not only an historic justification, but also a doctrinal foundation." Giordano Bruno Guerri, "Il teorico dell'attualismo che divenne ministro," *Il Giornale* (Milan), 19 February 2000, p. 5.
13. That is true for any empirical political system. It would be hard to argue that the political system of the United States satisfied the political vision of John Locke or David Hume. Even more difficult would it be to argue that Stalin's Soviet Union or Mao's China fully represented the philosophical and moral views of Karl Marx or Friedrich Engels.
14. Benedetto Gentile, *Giovanni Gentile dal discorso agli italiani alla morte*, p. 40.
15. A. James Gregor, *The Fascist Persuasion in Radical Politics* (Princeton: Princeton University Press, 1974).

16. In speaking of the responsibilities of Fascism, Mussolini referred to Italy as "poor and a late comer...." See Mussolini, "La reforma della scuola," *Oo*, 20, p. 130.
17. See, for example, Mussolini, "Per la vera pacificazione," *Oo*, 17, p. 295.
18. See the discussion in Gregor, *Phoenix*, chap. 2, and Gregor, *A Place in the Sun*, chap. 1.
19. See Gentile's discussion in "Stampa fascista e responsabilità di partito," *FC*, pp. 117–121, particularly p. 121.
20. See the discussion in Irving Louis Horowitz, *Taking Lives: Genocide and State Power* (New Brunswick, N.J.: Transaction Press, 1997), chaps. 9 and 10.
21. I have argued that "totalitarianism" should not be measured in terms of the utilization of terror or mass murder, but in terms of the political intention of the system. See Gregor, *Phoenix*, chap. 6.
22. See the discussion of the brutality that attended the end of the Second World War in Italy. See Mazzantini, *I balilla andarono a Salò*. See also the evidence of Italian behavior in Ethiopia, in James Dugan and Laurence Lafore, *Days of Emperor and Clown: The Italo-Ethiopian War 1935–1936* (New York: Doubleday, 1973), chap. 11.
23. National Socialism was equally collectivist, predicating its collectivism on racial psychology. See the discussion in Gregor, *Contemporary Radical Ideologies: Totalitarian Thought in the Twentieth Century* (New York: Random House, 1968), chap. 5.
24. See the discussion in Maria Hsia Chang, *Return of the Dragon: China's Wounded Nationalism* (Boulder, Colo.: Westview Press, 2001).
25. See the account in Gregor, *A Place in the Sun*.

Index